Influence of Hinduism on Indian Christian Theology

Interfaith Treasures Uncovered

Under this Series, the Publishers endeavor to focus on Comparative Studies pertaining to Christian Faith & Living in the central matrix and Hinduism, Buddhism, Sikhism, Islam, Judaism, etc., on the peripheral. The Studies shall cover topics like Literature & Poetry, Indigenous Philosophizing, Ethical response towards Agriculture, Health & Healing, Science & Technology, Ecofeminist Theology, Sociological approach towards Human Rights, Law & Politics, Arts, History of Ideas, Ancient Civilizations, Cultural Contiguity, Religious Cosmologies & Mysticism, Footsteps of famous Theologians, World Peace & Harmony, Global Capitalism, Network Marketing, Cybertheology, Population & Demographics, Epigraphic Studies, Contextualized Education, and many others. We welcome a Mss. on any topic/s mentioned, whether they are original works, scholarly monographs, collections of conference papers, revised dissertations, or translations of historical documents. Through the Series, we are striving to put forward published works that may help Institutions, Academic Bodies, Researchers, Scholars and the World at large in furthering their respective knowledge and understanding on the concerned subject. We welcome your comments on our efforts and further suggestions on how we can foster the upcoming books on parallel interfaces between and among Christianity and other religions.

Interfaith Treasures Uncovered - 10

Influence of Hinduism on Indian Christian Theology

A Critique Appropriating Panikkarian Trinity

Nannu K

CWI

Christian World Imprints™

First Published in 2018 by

Christian World Imprints(TM)
Christian Publishing & Books from India
H-12 Bali Nagar, **New Delhi-110015**
info@christianworldimprints.com
www.ChristianWorldImprints.com
Phone: +91 11 25465925

ISBN: 978-93-5148-203-1 (HB) ISBN: 978-93-5148-204-8 (PB)

Cataloging in Publication Data--DK
Courtesy: D.K. Agencies (P) Ltd. <docinfo@dkagencies.com>

Nannu, K., 1978- **author.**
Influence of Hinduism on Indian Christian theology : a critique appropriating Panikkarian trinity / Nannu K.
pages cm. -- (Interfaith treasures uncovered ; 10)
ISBN 9789351482031 (HB)
ISBN 9789351482048 (PB)

1. Panikkar, Raimon, 1918-2010. 2. Theology of religions (Christian theology) 3. Christianity and other religions--Hinduism. 4. Hinduism--Relations--Christianity. 5. Trinity. I. Title. II. Series: Interfaith treasures uncovered ; 10.

BR128.H5N36 2018 DDC 261.245 23

Printed in India.

For The Glory of God
I Dedicate
this Book to

My Dear Parents

Contents

Foreword xiii
Acknowledgement xvii
List of Abbreviations xix
Introduction xxi

Chapter 1: Raimundo Panikkar: A Pilgrimage to Contemporary Theological Consciousness 1

1.0 Introduction 1
1.1 Memoir 2
1.1.1 Life and Career 2
1.1.2 Vision and Interest 3
1.2 The Context Formulated the Theological Thought of Panikkar 4
1.2.1 The Socio-Political Context 4
1.2.2 The Religio-Cultural Context 4
1.2.3 The Philosophical Context 5
1.2.4 Theological Context 5
1.3 Characteristics of Panikkar's Thought 5
1.3.1 Distinctively Christian 5
1.3.2 Comprehensively Ecumenical 6
1.3.3 Point of Departure 6
1.3.4 Coincidence of Opposites 6
1.3.5 Theology of Neo-logoism 7
1.4 Methodological Considerations 7
1.4.1 Quest for a Different Methodology 7
1.4.2 Homological Principle 8
1.4.3 Homeomorphic Equivalence 8

1.5 Methodological Pre-Suppositions 9
1.5.1 Reality as Radical Relativity 9
1.5.1.1 Theologism 10
1.5.1.2 Humanism 10
1.5.1.3 Theandrism 10
1.5.2 Tempiternity 11
1.5.3 Myth and Logos 11
1.5.4 Symbol 12
1.5.5 Faith 12
1.6 A Summary Presentation of Panikkar's Theological Thought 13
1.6.1 Theology of Religions 13
1.6.1.1 Understanding of Religion 13
1.6.1.2 Pluralism 14
1.6.2 Dialogue 15
1.6.2.1 Ecumenical Ecumenism 16
1.6.3 Church and Christianity 16
1.6.3.1 Church 16
1.6.3.2 Christianity 17
1.6.4 Christology 17
1.6.4.1 Ontic Christology 18
1.6.4.2 Christophany 18
1.6.5 Cosmotheandrism 20
1.6.5.1 Cosmotheandric Intuition 21
1.6.5.2 Ecosophy 22
1.7 Panikkar: A Pilgrimage 22
Conclusion 23

Chapter 2: Trinity and Hindu Spirituality: Panikkar's Triadic Synthesis 25
2.0. Introduction 25
2.1. Hindu Spirituality 26
2.1.1 Definition 26
2.1.1.1 Christian Interpretation 26
2.1.2 Development 28
2.1.3 Foundations 28
2.1.3.1 Reality 28
2.1.3.2 World 29

2.1.3.3 Human Life 29
2.1.3.4 Self or Soul 29
2.2 Hindu Spirituality as Margas 30
2.2.1 Karma Marga 30
2.2.2 Bhakti Marga 31
2.2.3 Jnana Marga 31
2.3 Panikkarian Trinity 32
2.3.1 Indian Theological Understanding 32
2.3.2 Basic Pre-Suppositions 32
2.3.3 Formative Factors 34
2.3.3.1 Pluriform of Religious Settings 34
2.3.3.2 Eastern Influence 34
2.3.3.3 Comparative Religious Hermeneutics 35
2.3.3.4 Methodological Questions 35
2.4 Triadic Synthesis of Panikkar 36
2.4.1 Primary Synthesis 36
2.4.2 Secondary Synthesis 38
2.4.3 Tertiary Synthesis 39
2.5 Trinity or Theandrism 39
2.6 Basic Deviations 41
2.6.1 Nihilism 42
2.6.2 Humanism 42
2.6.3 Angelism 42
Conclusion 43

Chapter 3: Influence of Hinduism on Panikkar's Theology 45
3.0 Introduction 45
3.1 Perception of Hinduism 45
3.1.1 Insight on Religion 45
3.1.2 Understanding of Hinduism 46
3.1.2.1 Relationship between Hinduism and Christianity 46
3.1.2.2 The Most Penetrating Question 48
3.2 Inclusion of Hindu Religious Thought 48
3.2.1 The Idea of Integration 49
3.2.2 Necessitated Conditions of Integration 49
3.2.3 Principles of Integration 49
3.2.4 Trinitarian Integration 50

3.3 Legitimization 50
3.3.1 Common Ground for Christian and Non-Christian Collaboration: A Proposal 50
3.3.1.1 Koinonia 51
3.3.1.2 Diakonia 51
3.3.1.3 Kerygma 51
3.3.2 Non-Christian Surroundings: Panikkar's Claims 52
3.3.2.1 Critique of the Christian Attitude 52
3.3.2.2 Alternative 53
3.4 Influence of Hinduism 54
3.4.1 Influence of Advaitic Hinduism 54
3.4.1.1 Advaita 54
3.4.1.2 Panikkar's Re-Interpretation of Advaita Vedanta 54
3.4.1.3 Influence of Advaitic Spirituality an Panikkar 55
3.4.2 Hindu Religious Monograms: Philosophical/Vedantic Influence 57
3.4.2.1 Meaning of Monograms in Theology 57
3.4.2.2 Brahman 58
3.4.2.3 Atman 59
3.4.2.4 Isvara 59
3.4.2.5 Samdhya 61
3.4.3 Influence of Bhagavat Gita 61
3.4.4 Upanishadic Influence 62
3.5 Hindu-Christian Theology: Panikkar's Query 62
Conclusion 63

Chapter 4: A Subaltern Critique on Hindu Hegemonic Theology of Panikkar 65
4.0 Introducton 65
4.1 Subaltern Critique 65
4.1.1 The Term Subaltern 65
4.1.2 Subaltern Critique 66
4.1.2.1 Subaltern Critique: Integration or Autonomy 67
4.1.3 Subaltern Hermeneutics 68

4.1.3.1 Subaltern Hermeneutics as Post Colonial Deconstruction 68
4.1.4 Subaltern Critique on Religion and Hinduism 69
4.2 Panikkar's Hindu Hegemonic Theology 70
4.2.1 Hinduized Theology 71
4.2.2 Allegations 72
4.2.3 Can Panikkar's Theology be Astika? 73
4.2.3.1 Panikkar's Theology – Theology from 'Above' 73
4.2.4 Why Did Panikkar not Use Subaltern Religion for Theologizing? 74
4.3 Critique on Panikkar's Hindu Hegemonic Theology 74
4.3.1 Panikkar's Methodology 75
4.3.1.1 Subaltern Methodology 76
4.3.2 Panikkar's Theological Framework 77
4.3.2.1 Hindu Spirituality Vs Subaltern Spirituality 78
4.3.3 Theological Verbalization 79
4.3.3.1 Christology: The Point of Departure 79
4.3.3.2 Brahman – God 81
4.3.3.3 Advaita Vedanta 82
4.3.3.4 Atman 83
4.3.4 Critique on Dharma 84
4.4 Does Panikkar's Theology Really Gasp for Breath? 84
4.4.1 Indian Christian Theology at the Intersection 85
4.4.2 From Latin Captivity to Brahmanic Captivity 87
4.5 Towards Life – Centric Theology 88
Conclusion 90

General Conclusion 93

Bibliography 97

Foreword

Authentic interpretation of Christian faith, which is precisely the task of any theological enterprise, takes place when one reflects on Christian faith in the given context, giving due consideration to all its needs and resources available there. New Testament records few early Christian attempts to articulate Christian faith using the resources available from the context. St. Paul, in his speech at Athens (Acts 17), preferred to use insights from Greek poets and philosophers, rather than from Jewish thinkers or scriptures, to effectively communicate the Gospel to an audience steeped in Greek philosophy. A similar attempt was made by the author of John's Gospel when the concept of logos was creatively used in constructing a relevant Christology by the fusion of Jewish, Greek and Christian ideas regarding the logos. The history of Christian thought bears witness to the fact that Christian theological formulations has always been influenced by the context. Greek philosophical background of Alexandria had a great influence on early Christian thinkers.

In India also the philosophical and religious traditions of the Indian context have been used as resources for theologizing. However, the resources available in 'little traditions' and oral traditions were not taken seriously in the major works of Indian Christian Theology till recently. Nannu's treatment of Panikkar's theology powerfully illustrates this point. Employing post-colonial lenses of subaltern hermeneutics, he critiques the bold theological explorations of Panikkar, on the one hand and gives due importance to his innovate ways of theologizing in the Indian context, on the other.

The author's assessment of the theology of Panikkar in the backdrop of his philosophical and cultural moorings has brought out the influence of priestly Hinduism in his theology. Through this he was able to show how Panikkar creatively mixed the Hindu and Christian ideas and at the same time warns us about the dangers of a Hinduised theology. The author's concern for maintaining the distinctiveness and sanctity of Christian theology in the pluralistic context of India deserves appreciation. This work cautions every Indian Christian theologian of the problems involved in using the resources available in one's context. It is important to take seriously the distinctive soteriological paradigms of different religious traditions when one uses concepts from other religious traditions.

Nannu has opened up a new path of theologizing which is not travelled by many Indian theologians. Following the lines of eminent theologians, such as M. M. Thomas, who suggested that articulation of Christian faith in our context means to theologise in the context plurality of religions and cultures, Nannu underlines the need to take the plurality of Indian context seriously in our Theology. However, it is important to take into serious consideration not only the 'great traditions' of our context, but also the neglected 'little traditions' that give expression to the aspirations and hopes of a great majority of Indian population. Nannu has done well to draw our attention to this need in Indian Christian Theology. His stress on foregrounding the pressing needs of the context, especially that of the Dalits and the marginalized as well as employing the resources available from such a context of the marginalized for articulating Christian faith are to be taken seriously by every Indian Christian Theologian.

The method employed by the author for making a critical assessment of Panikkar is also noteworthy. He used the post-colonial insights quite judiciously and effectively for his purposes. Nannu has shown that suitable hermeneutical tools can be productively used for theologizing in our context. This book gives the impression that the tools of interpretation of Christian faith emerges from the kind of context from which one theologizes.

Thus, this book is an eye-opener to every theologian who ventures to use the resources available in one's context. Although, it presents before budding Indian Theologians immense possibilities of the varied and rich resources of our context, it warns them of the dangers in the use of resources from different cultural and religious traditions. It also offers us the possibilities of making creative use of critical tools available outside one's context to serve the purposes of one's context. It is refreshing to note that Nannu's work emphasizes the need to preserve the integrity and distinctiveness in Christian theological enterprise, remaining faithful to the Christian tradition, while one engages in creative hermeneutical ventures in one's context.

Dr. Sam Peedikayil Mathew
Research Coordinator
SHUATS, Allahabad

Acknowledgement

I thank God, the Almighty, for helping me all through my theological pursuit, especially in doing this work.

I put into words my hearty thanks to Rev. Dr. Ivy Singh, my adviser and professor, for her inevitable suggestions and precious supervision in lengthening my thoughts and views in getting this work done.

I am grateful to Dr. Sam P. Mathew for taking out his precious time in writing the foreword for the book.

I am thankful to the former principal, Rev. Dr. Mohan Larbeer, the principal, Rev. Dr. Gnanavaram, P. G. Dean, Rev. Dr. M. Singh, and faculty members, for their concerns during my studies.

I am obliged to my parents, Mr. M. Kuttan and Mrs. R. Lalitha for their priceless prayers and for being an immense brainwave in my theological venture and being an admirable support during my studies.

I express my gratitude to my brothers and sisters, brother-in-law, sisters-in-law and their sons and daughters, for their unrelenting love and encouragement for studies.

I am deeply indebted to Pr. C. Johnson and family, and my local church members for cheering me in my ministerial configuration and studies.

I would like to record my gratitude to parents-in-law, brothers-in-law, sisters-in-law, their families and their son and daughter for their care, prayers and concerns towards my studies.

My heartfelt thanks to the librarians and staff of the libraries of the TTS, Madurai; FFRRC, Kottayam; and FTS, Manakala.

I thank all my friends, especially Rev. L. J. Samjis, Issac Jabalal, Laji Chacko, N. Jesin, Prakash James, Parakash Nayagam and Eugine Skaria for their commendable support and impressive motivation in my studies.

My open thanks to Mrs. Gayathri Basker who helped me in bringing out this work proficiently.

At the most, I am grateful to my beloved wife, Gifty and my two children, Jesna and Jeswin, for their love, concern, endurance, prayer, optimism and jollity in my life studies as well, especially in getting this work successfully done.

List of Abbreviations

AJT	*Asian Journal of Theology*
Cf	Confer (Compare)
CTC	*Christian Conference of Asia Theological concerns*
EATWOT	Ecumenical Association of Third World Theologians
Ed	Editor
Eds	Editors
Eph	Ephesians
HTR	*Harvard Theological Review*
Ibid	ibidem (Same Source)
JICPR	*Journal of Indian Council of Philosophical Research*
JPJRS	*Jnanadeepa: Pune Journal of Religious Studies*
n.	notes (referring to foot notes)
n.d	no date of publication given
n.p	no place of publication
NCCR	*National Council of Churches Review*
RC	Roman Catholic Church
Sic	thus (to indicate error in a quoted Passage)
Trans	Translator
VJTR	*Vidhya Jyoti Journal of Theological Reflection*
Vol	Volume
Vs	(Versus) against
YHWH	Yahweh

Introduction

Panikkar's theology is now being increasingly referred to as the 'Hinduized theology'. For the influence of Hinduism on Indian Christian theology is not a new phenomenon for there is a pressing need to stimulate the people to find the common basis for various religions, and establish religious co- ordination, harmony and peace[1]. This research, therefore, is an attempt to point out the *influence of Hinduism on Panikkar's Theology of Trinity* because the Christian Theology is greatly influenced by the corresponding Hinduism time to time. Hence, theology of Panikkar is a fascinating mixture of both Christian and Hindu traditions which seeks to explore Christian theology purposefully Indian in its thought pattern, theological terminology and general sensitivity to the Indian culture.

Background of the Research

Panikkar's theology of trinity is based on the Interculturation/ homeomorphic methodology which tries to homogenize trinity with Hindu spiritualities. As it explains in relation to the framework of Hindu spiritualities, he was highly influenced by priestly Hinduism/ Brahmanic traditions and thereby it solely conveys reductionalistic approach on the study of Christian trinity. Therefore, there is a critical need to respond to this issue theologically and thus this research seeks to address the dangers of Hinduized trinity and to preserve the sanctity of Indian Christian Theology.

---

[1] V. W. Deshpande, *The Impact of Ancient Indian Thought on Christianity* (Delhi: A.P.H. Publishing Corp., 1996), v.

Exploring the Research

Raimundo Panikkar is an eminent Roman Catholic theologian who has been associated with the Universities in India and abroad as well. His field of study is the relation between theology and religions, preferably between Christianity and Hinduism. Therefore, it is impossible to examine the theology of Panikkar without being impressed by his indebtedness to Hinduism. The concept of trinity and world religions occupy a predominant place in the movement of Indian Christian Theology which by and by tends to use Hinduism as its chief point of reference.

In this regard, Panikkar is more inclined to Brahmanic religion in a way that he elucidates the doctrine of trinity in par with Hindu spirituality as he connects Karma marga with the spirituality of the Father Bhakti marga with the spiritruality of the Son and Jnana marga with the spirituality of the Holy Spirit. It shows that Panikkar interprets Christian trinity on the basis of Interculturation methodology which tries to find a correlation of functions between distinct religious traditions. Currently, this attempt in theology is seen as a forms of dangerous 'Brahmanic hegemony'[2] or 'Sanskrit Captivity'.[3]

At time passed by, Indian liberation theologians made scathing attack on this Hindu hegemonic theology. A. P. Nirmal criticized that the classical Indian Christian theology is primarily in line with the Brahmanic traditions of India.[4] Others criticized this new tendency as seeking to Christianize Hinduism or Hinduize Christianity[5] whereas Panikkar uses only Hindu philosophical and religious categories (Brahminical Hinduism) for interpreting Christian theology.

---

[2] Eric J. Lott, "Hindu Theology's Forgotten Struggles" in Israel Selvanayagam (ed.), *Moving Forms of Theology: Faith Talk's Changing Contexts* (Delhi: ISPCK, 2002), 76.

[3] Israel Selvanayagam, "Water of Life and Indian Cups: Protestant Attempts at Theologizing in India" in Sebastian C. H. Kim (ed.), *Christian Theology in Asia* (New York: Cambridge University Press, 2008), 65.

[4] A. P. Nirmal, "Towards a Christian Theology" in James Massey (ed.), *Indigenous People: Dalits* (Delhi: ISPCK, 1994), 215.

[5] Timothy C. Tennet, *Building Christianity on Indian Foundations* (Delhi: ISPCK, 2000), 2.

Researcher, therefore, feels it is the prime time to re-examine, to re-interpret and interrogate the theology of Panikkar on the grounds of subaltern perspective, because Godhead must be released from the various forms of Hindu hegemonic propensity. Instead of recognizing subaltern traditions, life experience, pathos, pain and suffering Panikkar's theology suppresses all these and makes tirelessly Christian theology the 'prisoner' of Hindu speculation.

Definitions

Hinduism: Literally Hinduism is the title applied to that of a religion which prevails among the vast majority of the present population of the Indian nation. By Hinduism, W. Crooke means, Brahmanic Hinduism which is the term generally used to designate the higher and more philosophical form of Hinduism.[6] The same meaning is taken by the author for this work.

Trinity: Theologically, Christian doctrine of trinity-the teaching that one God is eternally three distinct persons, the Father (sic), the Son and the Holy Spirit.[7] In speaking divine trinity, therefore, a peculiar kind of unity is mentioned, namely, a unity that is trinal. But Panikkar's trinity is incoherent of this unity since it is utterly related to tri-margas: Karma, Jnana and Bhakti.

Significace of the Research

Christians in India generally ask about the Christian influence on other faiths or religions; but rarely have they raised the questions as to how far the other faiths have influenced Christian livings in India. It is hard to imagine that in a country where approximately 85% of the people profess Hindu faith, Christians who constitute only about 2.5% of the population, are totally free from possible Hindu influence. An explorative enquiry into the Hindu influence on Christian theology in India is, therefore, indispensible. It is also significant if Christian theology be freed Hindu Hegemonism and it tries to incorporate Asian realities into consideration.

---

[6] W. Crooke, "Hinduism" in James Hastings (ed.), *Encyclopedia of Religion and Ethics,* Vol.VI (Edinburg: T&T Clark, 1974), 686.

[7] Bruce D. Marshall, "Trinity" in Gareth Jones (ed.), *The Blackwell Companion to Modern Theology* (UK: Blackwell Publishing, 2007), 183.

Scope and Limitation

The scope of this research has been limited to an analysis and critique of his theology of trinity. Accordingly, this study is limited to Hindu spirituality not Hinduism in general. For Hindu spirituality is the basis on which Panikkar builds theology of trinity. Having given importance to subalterns, this critique is exclusively limited to Panikkar's methodology, framework and theological elucidation.

Methodology Adopted

Considering the great important of the research methods, the researcher has selected analytic-critical method for this work. Explorative analysis is extensively used to restrain researcher to avoid both eccentric conclusions and to get a systematic investigation and examination of the subject. Critical method is introduced to assess the intensity of Panikkar's influence on Hinduism which is purely based on subaltern perspective. The methodic tool of inter-disciplinary has been employed by the researcher, for it has drawn tools and insights from various realms-Christian Trinity, Hinduism Indian Philosophy, Subaltern Studies, and Hermeneutics etc. The methodological device of critique-creativity has widely been used in the analysis. Critique is negatively employed and creativity is positively introduced, to deconstruct and reconstruct respectively.

Sources of the Research

The present research is based on the library sources for both primary and secondary sources. The literary output on Panikkar's thought in general and his seminal books and articles (in journals and books) are hard-hittingly considered by the author.

Previous Research

There have been sufficient research works done on Panikkar which cover some of the aspects related to this topic. Preferably, in 1987 Dominic Veliath published his doctoral dissertation entitled *Theological Approach and Understanding of Religion* in which he tried to bring out whole theological thought of Panikkar. He has also written two articles: the first one is related to Panikkar's theological framework that is entitled *From Ontonomy to Dialogical Dialogue* in *Vidhyajyothi* (March-2002) and the other article is more related to Panikkar's understanding on trinity which is entitled *The Trinity in Indian Theology* in *Kristhu Jyoti* (June-1992). Joseph Prabhu's (ed.), *The Intercultural Challenge of Raimon Panikkar* (1996), Anto Karokaran's *Raymond Panikkar's Theology of Religions: A Critique* in *VJTR* (October-1994), Biren Kumar Nayak, *"A Critical Study of Christology of Raimundo Panikkar in an Advaitic framework"* in *Bangalore Theological Forum, (*Dec 2006) and Dankfreed Reetz's, "*R. Panikkar's Theology of Religions"* in *Religion and Society* (Semptember-1968) are other notable works which provide an ample basis to know his views and thought.

This research, however, differs from the previous in dealing with the critique on trinity from the subaltern perspective. Subaltern critique, therefore, is the major thrust of this research and thereby it formulates a comprehensive view of the problem enabling a critical response and makes the Christian community discern the need, to be faithful towards subaltern religions from the emerging declension.

Plan of the Research

The research is presented in four chapters: The first chapter undertakes Panikkar's life sketch, life setting, nature and characteristic of his theology, methodological consideration and summary presentation of his theological thought. Having gathered together the main elements of Panikkar's thought, researcher notices a shift in his perspective, in his theologizing process notably its relation to other religions. In the initial stages of his reflection, the uniqueness of Christianity as against other religions is stressed, in the latter stages; he is an itinerary in his dialogical perspective of thought. Thus, Panikkar's theology has taken evolutionary phases, moving from an exclusivistic stance through inclusivism to pluralism and Panikkar's over all indebtedness to Hinduism in theologizing is predominantly articulated. Hence, Panikkar is characterized as a pilgrimage to contemporary theological consciousness.

With an overview of Panikkar's theological thought, the second chapter discusses about his triadic synthesis that is between Hindu spiritualities and Christian trinity. For centuries, Christian theologians have been constantly perplexed and inspired as well by the doctrine of trinity. Countless philosophical attempts tried to balance the trinity. One among them was Panikkar who introduced Advaitin color to trinity to the theological world. The pioneers of Indian ashram movement, as we see, have great liking for *Sat-Cit-Ananda* as Indian expression of trinity. Panikkar studiously avoids this terminology and finds his clue in the traditional types of spiritualities or *margas* of Hinduism: *Karma, Bhakti and Jnana.* Through which he wants to show that Christianity has no monopoly on Trinitarianism and shows that the Trinitarian claims of Christianity can be enriched by the contributions of different traditions. What the author has suggested is that, it is not Christian imperialism but *Hindu Hegemonism* by which Christian tradition is subsumed under the Hindu categories and this defect must be overcome.

Having been discussed his understanding of trinity, the third chapter probes into the possibilities for making subaltern critique stronger. In India, there has been an attempt to state the Christian faith in Indian terms and thought patterns. Epistemologically, doctrine of God is one of the prime areas in which some theological frameworks have taken place. However, their approach to the problem of the nature of God is divided along the lines of various Hindu philosophical traditions, notably Advaita. Likewise Panikkar's theology of trinity has radically been influenced by the Brahmanic tradition of Hinduism thereby his Trinitarian theology is purely Advaitic or Brahmanic. Nevertheless, Panikkar's trintarian theology merits a distinctively oriental and most appropriately Hindu adjective. His wrong use of integration may lead to syncretism which continues to be the problem as long as Christ is in the scene thus inevitably we Christianize or we Hinduize it. While this is the case, the doctrine of trinity is irrelevant for the subalterns who are more or less free from the so called Brahmanic traditions. In short Panikkar is advocating a lukewarm interpretation of any tradition and a dilution of the incisiveness of any religion.

As the author wants to take up the discussion further to reflect critically, the fourth chapter makes a critical evaluation on Panikkar's theology which is based on subaltern paradigm. India needs a living theology which addresses itself to the questions, quests, vibes and sufferings of a people in a context. Panikkar's theology excludes these realities and perpetuates Hindu hegemonic theology. It seems that Panikkar's pluralistic paradigm and dialogical methodology lead one to domestication or trivialization or privatization of Christian faith. By leaving the inherited ancestral paradigm and its models aside, a few Indian theologians audaciously sought for new paths that respond adequately to the Indian situations and needs that are embedded in the local culture. It is important to note that the religious world of the Dalits and marginalized can be re-collected and remembered. This unanimously proves the fact that Panikkar's theology is really gasping for breath from Brahmanic capitivity. Thus, the research ends by questioning Panikkar's theological position and concludes that he is extremely predisposed by Hinduism than any other religions in India.

Chapter 1

Raimundo Panikkar
A Pilgrimage to Contemporary Theological Consciousness

1.0 Introduction

Raimundo Panikkar[8] is best known as one of the pioneers and most creative theologians in the field of interreligious and intercultural encounter. Panikkar developed his theological thought from the perspective of four worlds in all of which he is at home: the Christian in which he was brought up, the Hindu, the world of his father, the Buddhist and the modern secular world. His contributions, therefore, range over various fields such as Philosophy of Science, Theology, Religious Studies, Cultural History, Indology, Mysticism, Scriptural Exegesis, Spirituality and Politics. As a profound thinker Panikkar's sole theological consciousness is to build up an Indian interpretation of Christian revelation or a Christian interpretation of Hinduism for which he moves from one to another constantly. The focus of this chapter is on the formative factors of Panikkar's theological thought

[8] His name is written in three ways: Raimundo Panikkar, Raymond Panikkar and Raimon Panikkar.

which immensively relates between Christianity and Hinduism and builds a bridge on plurality of religions. Primarily it presents the biography of Panikkar, context of his thought, his basic presuppositions, methodological considerations and characteristics of his thought. It also unfolds the brief summary of his theological thought.

1.1 Memoir

Contemporary theologians characterize Panikkar differently; E. H. Cousins describes him as "one who has stood on the boundary, not primarily between religion and culture but between diverse culture themselves in their religious depth."[9] B. Nelson characterizes him as "A New Science of Civilizational Analysis."[10] E. H. Cousins again aptly styled Panikkar as "the child of diverse cultures and the academic product of several disciplines."[11] Mean while Anthoniraj Thumma qualifies him as "an apostle of dialogue."[12]

1.1.1 Life and Career

Raimundo Panikkar was born as the son of a Catholic Catalan and a Hindu Indian. His mother was a well-educated daughter of the Catalan bourgeoisie; his father derived from an upper caste Malabar Nair family from South India (Kerala). Panikkar's father was a freedom fighter during British colonial rule in India and escaped from Britain and married into a Catalan family. Panikkar's father studied in England and was the representative of a German chemical company in Barcelona. Educated at a Jesuit school, Panikkar studied Chemistry and Philosophy at the universities of Barcelona, Bonn and Madrid, and Catholic Theology in Madrid and Rome.

---

[9] Dominic Veliath, *Theological Approach and Understanding of Religions- Jean Danielou and Raimundo Panikkar: A Study in Contrast* (Bangalore: Kristu Jyothi College, 1998), 81. Cited from, E. H. Cousins, "Introduction: Panikkar Symposium at Santa Barbara", *Cross Currents* (Summer- 1979), 131.

[10] *Ibid. Cited from, B. Nelson,* "A New Scientific Civilizational Analysis: A Tribute to Panikkar", *Cross Currents* (Summer- 1979), 135.

[11] *Ibid. Cited from,* E. H. Cousins, "Introduction: Panikkar Symposium at Santa Barbara", *Cross Currents* (Summer- 1979), 132.

[12] Anthoni Raj Thumma, *Breaking Barriers: Liberation of Dialogue and Dialogue of Liberation* (Delhi: ISPCK, 2000), 1.

He holds doctorates in Philosophy (1945), Science (1958, both at Complutense University of Madrid) and Theology (1961, Pontifical Lateran University in Rome), and was professor at the Complutense University of Madrid (1946-53). He was ordained as a Catholic priest in 1946. In 1953, he left Europe for India where he undertook studies in Indian Philosophy and religion at the university of Mysore and Banaras Hindu University, and engaged in Hindu-Christian dialogue, with a short time as a professor in Rome (1962-63). From 1967-71, he held a professorship at Harvard university, and from 1971-78 he was a professor of Religious Studies at University of California, Santa Barbara.[13] Currently he lives in Tavertet, in the mountains of Catalonia outside Barcelona. Panikkar has written over 40 books and more than 900 articles.[14]

1.1.2 Vision and Interest

A. M. Mundadan rightly observed "like Paul Tillich, Panikkar has stood on the boundary... The boundary between the East and West, between Christianity and Hinduism, Buddhism and Secular Culture."[15] Panikkar could say that "thus I am at the confluence of *(sangama)* the four rivers: the Hindu, the Christian, the Buddhist and the Secular Traditions."[16]

Three areas into which Panikkar has given special attention: History of Religions, Theology and Hermeneutics. To promote the cross-cultural understanding he has made available to the public the philosophical and religious traditions of India. It by and by resulted in the publication of *The Vedic Experience- Mantramanjari (1977-78).* In the area of theology he is interpreting Christian doctrine in interreligious context. The three seminal works are; *The Unknown Christ of Hinduism (1964, 82), The Trinity and World Religions (1970)* and *The Trinity and the Religious Experience of Man (1973, 1975).*

---

[13] Hans Schwarz, *Theology in a Global Context* (Michigan: Grand Rapids, 2005), 526.

[14] *http://en.wikipedia.org/wiki/Raimon_Panikkar* (22 January-2010).

[15] A. M. Mundadan, *Paths of Indian Theology* (Bangalore: Dharmaram Publications, 1998), 92.

[16] Raimond Panikkar, *The Unknown Christ of Hinduism: Towards an Ecumenical Christophany* Revised Edition (Bangalore: ATC, 1982), x. (hereafter, R. Panikkar).

Panikkar is also a *founding father* of the prestigious *Castelli Conference* on hermeneutics at the University of Rome started in 1961.[17] *The Intra-Religious Dialogue (1978)* and *Myth, Faith and Hermeneutics: Cross Cultural Studies (1979)* are telling examples of his innovative cross cultural hermeneutic achievement.

1.2 The Context Formulated the Theological Thought of Panikkar

Panikkar's theological thought emerged in three phases: socio-political, religio-cultural and philosophical contexts which are discussed briefly in this section.

1.2.1 The Socio-Political Context

The church in India had to grapple with her God-given task in the changed climate of post independent India particularly for indigenous theology. Hence, the Catholic all India seminar on *The Church in India Today* declared that we urgently need a theology that is truly India in its categories of thought and in the situations that it envisages.[18] But it cannot be done even defined unless the Church takes into account the salvific value of the Major old religions (Buddhism & Hinduism) existing in a country like India. Panikkar appears in this scenario with the new meaning to the Christian theology and message.

1.2.2 The Religio-Cultural Context

Panikkar's theological thinking developed in the context of the plurality of the old religions and pluriform of cultures. B.K. Nayak opines that his own world of plurality prompted him to think pluralistically though he is brought up in the strictest orthodoxy of Christianity.[19] Panikkar outlines his thinking as follows; "the truths which the Christian doctrine, on the one hand and Hindu doctrine on the other propound as universal have often come to be thought

[17] A. M. Mundadan, *Paths of Indian Theology*, 94.

[18] Anto Karokaran, *Evangelization and Diakonia: A Study in the Indian Perspective* (Bangalore: Dharmaram Publication, 1978), 138.

[19] Biren Kumar Nayak, "A Critical Study of Christology of Raimundo Panikkar in an Advaitic Frame Work", *Bangalore Theological Forum*, 32/2 (Dec 2006): 197.

of as particular and limited if not bigoted points of view, whereas in actuality both are formulations, necessarily limited cultural factors of a more universal faith."[20]

1.2.3 The Philosophical Context

Panikkar's primary concern in theologizing emerged from the problem of theology of religious which stems out of the philosophy of religion. According to Robin Boyd the philosophy of religion is all religions are on the same level and can therefore be compared with each other in such way that certain principle common to them all can be isolated.[21] Similarly, to Panikkar no religion can alone contain the plentitude of truth and claim a monopoly over it.[22]

1.2.4 Theological Context

Panikkar's whole effort was not in isolation but in the footsteps of Indian thinkers (Theologians) of building a bridge between Christianity and Hinduism. Indian theologians like Swami Abhishiktananda and Jules Monchanin… as well as Brahmabandhab Upadhyay's theological thought in Vedanta might have influenced Panikkar in his theological thought.[23]

1.3 Characteristics of Panikkar's Thought

As he is signaling a paradigm change in theology and therefore, has to be understood and judged within it. Ewert Cousins in his article enumerates following characteristics of the theology of Panikkar.[24]

1.3.1 Distinctively Christian

It is attested by Panikkar himself that the agreement here should not be found in a common denominator which would be obtained

---

[20] R. Panikkar, *The Unknown Christ of Hinduism*, Revised Edition, 7.

[21] Robin Boyd, *Khrist Advaita: A Theology for India* (Madras: CLS, 1977), 10.

[22] Anto Karokaran, *Evangelization and Diakonia: A Study in the Indian Perspective,* 664.

[23] Biren Kumar Nayak, "A Critical Study of Christology of Raimundo Panikkar in an Advaitic Frame Work", 198.

[24] A. M. Mundadan, *Paths of Indian Theology,* 103. Cited from E. H. Cousins, "*Introduction: Panikkar Symposium at Santa Barbara*", 150-152.

by chopping of all that is positive, valuable and distinctive, agreeing only in what is irrelevant and banal. It is not found by giving up the theistic affirmations and emasculating the atheistic convictions but by transcending both without negating them.[25] The researcher disassociates with it for, Panikkar's theology cannot truly be Christian but syncretic form of both Christian and Hindu.

1.3.2 Comprehensively Ecumenical

His theology is ecumenical in the widest sense of the word and derives its vitality from the lived experiences of the authentic adherents of different religions rather than from their philosophical and dogmatic systems and structures.[26] That is why he speaks of an ecumenical ecumenism, an ecumenism that is really ecumenical, catholic, engaged in a dialogue and encounter between religions.[27]

1.3.3 Point of Departure

For Panikkar the point of departure is not philosophy but religious experience. That is typically exemplified in his book entitled *The Trinity and World Religions.*

1.3.4 Coincidence of Opposites

In his elaboration of theandrism, Panikkar is able to combine the opposites in a synthesis. In the doctrines of Trinity and Christ, he finds the ground and expression for both the archetypes of the void and of the fullness. The silence of the Father (Buddhist Nihilism) is balanced by the fullness of the Logos (Christian Realism); the transcendence of the Father is balanced by the immanence of the Spirit (Avatara).[28]

---

[25] R. Panikkar, *Trinity and Religious Experience of Man (*New York: Orbis Books, 1973), XIII.

[26] Anto Karakaran, "Raimond Panikkar's Theology of Religions: A critique", *Indian Missiological Review* 12/2 (June-1996): 21.

[27] R. Panikkar, *Trinity and Religious Experience of Man*, 65.

[28] A. M. Mundadan, *Paths of Indian Theology,* 106.

1.3.5 Theology of Neo-logoism

It is remarkably unique that Panikkar has contributed lot of vocabularies in the field of Christian theology. Some of them are listed below: *Logos Spermatikos* (Logos is already in a seed form but not germinated), *Locus Theologicus* (Locus of Theology), *Tempiternal* (Combination of both time and eternity), *Cosmotheandrism* (Universe, God and Human), *Ecumenically Ecumenical* (All cultures and religions along with the social realities of a given country must find integral place in the theology of that particular country).[29] *Dialogically Dialogical* (Theology is made integral and comprehensive by dialogue).[30] In relation to intra religious dialogue he uses the terms such as *Totalitarian Exclusiveness, Libertarian Equalitarianism, and Mutual Fecundation,* etc. and in line with theology of religions he also uses new vocabularies like *Radical Relativity, Ontonomy,* and *Theonomy,* etc.

1.4 Methodological Considerations

Panikkar has introduced several methodologies to address several theological issues. Here, the writer concerned only of his distinctive methodology which he applied in the interpretation of Trinity.

1.4.1 Quest for a Different Methodology

In India, we increasingly realize that there are various cultures and religions apart from Christianity, and Christians consider other religion as 'objects'. According to Anthony Savari Raj "it is not enough that we examine objects out there according to our point of view but we must also somehow incorporate these objects as subjects of understanding.[31] In this sense Panikkar thinks to follow new methodological tool which is known as diatopical hermeneutics which attempts to study and integrate the wisdom of various

---

[29] R. Panikkar, "Toward an Ecumenical Ecumenism" (Editorial), *Journal of Ecumenical Studies* 19 (1982): 782.

[30] Anthoni Raj Thumma, *Breaking Barriers: Liberation of Dialogue and Dialogue of Liberation*, 101.

[31] Anthony Savari Raj, "The Diatopical Hermeneutics: R. Panikkar's Responds to the scientific study of religions", *Journal of Dharma* 21/2 (April-June 1996): 198.

cultures and traditions which are spatially (*Topoi*) far apart and hence have no common cultural source.[32] He reveals his sole aim as follows: "I am not affirming that what Christ conveyed is the same or not the same message of Hinduism. I am making, however, a fundamental assumption."[33] Panikkar also points out insufficiency of dialectical method which is one particular way in which human seeks intelligibly and the governing principle here is the principle of non-contradiction: either or.[34] That is why he proposes new principle in his methodology which is known as homological principle.

1.4.2 Homological Principle

Panikkar consider it as the golden rule of hermeneutics namely that any interpretations given from outside a tradition have to meet all the requirements of and at least phenomenologically coincide with the self interpretations given from within.[35] In other words starting point of interpretation should be a common area of agreement. For Panikkar it is geometrical notion which stands for the correlation between point of two different systems in which one point is one system corresponds to a homologous point in the other.[36] He is using this principle in his methodology, homeomorphic equivalence.

1.4.3 Homeomorphic Equivalence

It literally means 'similar forms' which suggests there may be a correlation of functions between specific beliefs in distinct religious traditions. This is the method that Panikkar follows both in his

---

[32] He distinguishes it from the morphological hermeneutics which bridges a factual gap and from the diachronical hermeneutics which efforts at closing a temporal gap. *Ibid.* 199 Cited from Panikkar, "Cross Cultural Studies", *Monchanin* 8 (June-December: 1975): 14.

[33] R. Panikkar, "The Category of Growth in Comparative Religion: A Critical Self Examination", *HTR* 66/1 (January-1873): 115.

[34] Anthony Savari Raj, "The Diatopical Hermeneutics: R. Panikkar's Responds to the scientific study of religions", 199.

[35] Dominic Veliath, *Theological Approach and Understanding of Religions- Jean Danielou and Raimundo Panikkar: A Study in Contrast, 83.* Cited from R. Panikkar "Indology as a Cross Cultural Cataclyst", *Numen* Vol. XXIIX (December-1971): 175.

[36] *Ibid.*, R. Panikkar "Indology as a Cross Cultural Cataclyst", *Numen* Vol. XXIIX (Dec 1971): 177.

seminal works, *The Unknown Christ of Hinduism* and *Trinity and World Religions.* According to A. M. Mundadan "his spirituality based theology may herald a new trend in Christian theology. This could bring about a paradigm shift in the whole of theological methodology that may launch a new era in theology."[37] Panikkar himself acknowledged that ...both Christ and Isvara are interpreted according to their respective functions within their own tradition... .[38] He goes on to argue each religion is like galaxy, simultaneously shaping its own criteria of thinking and its own criteria of truth and reality as well. In order therefore, to draw valid comparisons one must come to acknowledge what I call homeomorphic equivalent.[39] For him "an exposition of Christian mysteries utilizing Indian or other concepts and images, on the one hand, and interpretations of the religions of the world by means of Christian's concepts, on the other, would be important if I were engaged in the defense of a particular doctrine."[40] Thus, basic theologizing process of Panikkar is centered on the axis of Interculturation/homeomorphic equivalence. 'By homeomorphic equivalent I mean a third degree analogy which uncovers corresponding functions in the respective systems'.[41]

1.5 Methodological Pre-Suppositions

This topic exclusively deals with key categories and principles which characterize the methodological position of Panikkar.

1.5.1 Reality as Radical Relativity

Panikkar understood reality as radical relativity in the context of the fundamental issue which has challenged the human intelligence

---

[37] A. M. Mundadan, *Paths of Indian Theology,* 106.

[38] R. Panikkar, *The Unknown Christ of Hinduism,* Revised Edition, 147.

[39] R. Panikkar, "The Encounter of Religions: The Unavoidable Dialogue", *Janadeepa* 3/2 (July-2000): 164.

[40] R. Panikkar, "The Category of Growth in Comparative Religion: A Critical Self Examination", 115.

[41] *Ibid.*

through the centuries that is the problem of *one* and the *many.*[42] The different solutions proposed can be classified in to three types.

1.5.1.1Theologism

Panikkar calls this specific world vision as *heteronomy* which underscores the contingency of beings as having their basis in another.[43] Here beings are absolutely dependent on God and thereby one of the characteristics of this view is the absoluteness and transcendence of God.

1.5.1.2 Humanism

Panikkar calls it as *autonomy* that affirms the total independence of being. It has negative aspect that is it can lead to pantheism in so far as it identifies God and the world and to atheism, as a positive consideration of being as self sufficient.[44]

1.5.1.3 Theandrism

Panikkar term it as *ontonomy* which hinges on a basic understanding of the relationship between God and the world. It suggests that beings on the one hand, are not God, and on the other hand they are not not-God.[45] Thus, Panikkar argues that being is not isolated but ontologically related. At this juncture he alludes to the Advaita, God and world cannot be called two nor are they one as in the latter instance the world would vanish- hence non dualism.[46]

Panikkar concludes that ...reality is the radical relativity of all things, it shows the divine neither as one aspect of things nor as pure totality or otherness; but as the pure act and reality infinite mutual relatedness of everything... He is the very relationship, the radical

---

[42] Dominic Veliath, "From Ontonomy to Dialogical: A Passacoglia", *VJTR* 66/3 (March-2002): 196.

[43] *Ibid.*

[44] *Ibid.*, 197.

[45] Dominic Veliath, *Theological Approach and Understanding of Religions- Jean Danielou and Raimundo Panikkar: A Study in Contrast,* 87.

[46] *Ibid.* Cited from Panikkar, "la Demitologizzazione nel' Incontro del Christianesimo con I' Induismo" *ll problema della Demitizzazione Archivio di Filosofia* (1961): 245.

relativity, the non dualistic dimension, ground, summit or whatever we may choose according to our system of reference.[47] Similar way of thought is reflected on trinity and Cosmotheandrism. Former explains radical relativity and latter concerned of intuition.

1.5.2 Tempiternity

In *Worship and Secular Man* Panikkar elaborates the nature of Tempiternity in contrast to eternity and temporality. Panikkar connects eternity to a heteronomic conception of the world, temporality to an autonomic conception of the world and Tempiternity is the metaphysical locus of the theandric ontonomy. Tempiternity, as its very name would like to suggest, is neither eternity (an objectified notion belonging exclusively to God) nor temporality (subjective concept and the monopoly of the human being). As Panikkar writes: "I have created the word Tempiternity to express that which overcomes the scheme of time here and eternity later. I think that entire reality is Tempiternal that is temporal and eternal in one and the same time in a non-dualistic realm."[48]

1.5.3 Myth and Logos

Myth and Logos are two attempts of man (sic) to furnish an integral expression of reality. When one approach the myth with the instrument of Logos, the myth becomes mythology which signifies the death of the myth, because the myth is not an object but an instrument of knowledge, a fundamental human stance which cannot be scrutinized in the light of Logos.[49] For Panikkar any experience-sensory, intellectual or spiritual in fact functions as a myth.[50] He goes on to argue that there is no Logos without myth nor myth without Logos. In every Logos there is a myth, the myth that the logos says.

---

[47] R. Panikkar, "God of Silence", *Indian Journal of Theology* 21 (1972): 123-124.

[48] R. Panikkar, *Worship and Secular Man* (London: Orbis Books, 1973), 40.

[49] Dominic Veliath, *Theological Approach and Understanding of Religions- Jean Danielou and Raimundo Panikkar; A Study in Contrast,* 98.

[50] R. Panikkar, *Myth, Faith and Hermeneutics: Cross Cultural Studies* (Bangalore: ATC, 1983), 296.

In every myth there is Logos, the logos that tells the myth.[51] In short human awareness cannot be reduced to logical awareness, there is besides, also mythical awareness. In other words, myth is frame of reference and Logos is the thought or logical reason.

1.5.4 Symbol

Panikkar observes that "beings are in a certain manner, a symbol of God. Nature is the sign and symbol of the invisible reality."[52] The symbol is not another reality but the reality itself, the reality revealed. According to Panikkar, "Symbols stand for the entire reality as it appears and manifests itself through its manifold structure. The symbol is not the thing in itself, as this could be a mental abstraction, but the thing as it appears and manifests itself."[53]

In *Worship and Secular Man* the distinction between sign and symbols is underscored. Sign is what Panikkar calls an 'epistemic reality'; the symbol is neither a substitutive for the thing in itself but the very reality as it appears and manifests itself.[54] In other words symbol is ontological and metaphysical order and sign is epistemological reality. The symbol is neither a merely objective entity in the world, nor it a purely subjective entity in the mind. The symbol encompasses and constitutively links the two poles: the object and the subject (Mediator between myth and logos).[55]

1.5.5 Faith

His article namely, *Faith- Constitutive Dimension of Man* elaboratively discusses on faith. There have been variations in his understanding on faith. At the outset he had traditional stance then he moves to philosophical sense of faith. He understands that faith is a constitutive dimension of man (sic); distinguishing man (sic) from other beings...

---

[51] R. Panikkar, *Trinity and Religious Experience of Man,* ix.

[52] Dominic Veliath, *Theological Approach and Understanding of Religions- Jean Danielou and Raimundo Panikkar; A Study in Contrast,* 102. Cited from "Vision de Sintesis del Universo", *Humanismo Y Cruz,* 43.

[53] R. Panikkar, *Myth, Faith and Hermeneutics: Cross Cultural Studies,* 301.

[54] R. Panikkar, *Worship and Secular Man,* 20.

[55] R. Panikkar, *Myth, Faith and Hermeneutics: Cross Cultural Studies,* 7.

Faith is the ontological relation to the Absolute.[56] It is also admitted that faith has an intellectual dimension where he asks only those who have faith are saved...[57] He speaks of three areas of faith: ***firstly***, orthodoxy which helps one to doctrinal formulations, Panikkar calls it as belief which is the crystallization of.[58] ***Secondly,*** orthopoiesis which highlight the practical and volitive element in faith such as love and taking a life- decision. ***Finally,*** orthopraxis explains his/her belief. Panikkar also argues that beliefs are multifarious and necessarily pluralistic and he criticizes that a belief which does not always point to a 'beyond' is not belief but fanaticism.[59]

1.6 A Summary Presentation of Panikkar's Theological Thought

This will be done under the following heads: theology of religions, dialogue, church and Christianity, Christology, Cosmotheandrism, etc.

1.6.1 Theology of Religions

1.6.1.1 Understanding of Religion

Panikkar holds that no religion can contain the plentitude of truth and claim its monopoly. His Idea of religion seems to be the starting point of this theology; for, Panikkar distinguishes three levels in all religions; the sociological, sacramental and mysterious. In the sociological level all religions are equal and in the sacramental level they are complimentary. The level of mystery is distinguished from the other two, which are the means to have an access to the level of mystery.[60] Panikkar also establishes the functional equality of all religions in that all can lead their respective adherents to salvation. This idea is predominant in his seminal works, *The Unknown Christ of Hinduism and Trinity and World Religions.*

---

[56] R. Panikkar, "Faith- Constitutive Dimension of Man", *Journal of Ecumenical Studies* 8 (Spring- 1971): 227.

[57] *Ibid.*

[58] R. Panikkar, *Worship and Secular Man,* 9.

[59] R. Panikkar, "Faith and Belief: A Multifarious Experience", *Anglican Theological Review* 53 (1971): 323.

[60] R. Panikkar and Koothottil, "Man and Religion: A Dialogue with Panikkar", *Jeevadhara* 11 (1981): 16.

1.6.1.2 Pluralism

In so far as Panikkar's theology of religions is concerned, he explains in three expressions: the recognition of the fact of plurality, the tolerance of diversity of pluralism and pluralism.[61] Panikkar's theology of pluralism is summarized by O. V. Jathana as follows; pluralism is not just plurality, plurality is a phenomenological fact. Pluralism is... a critical attitude in the context of plurality with the realization that plurality cannot be reduced to one truth, as every truth has its own field and boundaries... It is not blind to error or evil, but it doesn't absolutizes any position...[62] Panikkar affirmed that ...pluralism adopts a non dualistic, advaitic, attitude that defends the pluralism of truth because reality itself is pluralistic... The mystery of trinity is the ultimate foundation for pluralism.[63] Panikkar is a critic of Copernican Revolution in theology and proposed the model called *Concentric Solar System.* He argues that centre is neither earth (one particular religion) nor the sun (God)... rather each solar system has its own centre and every galaxy turns reciprocally round the other. There is no absolute centre. Reality itself is concentric in as much as each being (each tradition) is the centre of the universe- of its own to begin with.[64] To sum up theology of religions of Panikkar is the living encounter of Christianity with Hinduism and other religions.[65] His theology of religion is a sheer syncretism. Amos Young clarifies that

---

[61] R. Panikkar, "Indic Christian Theology of Religious Pluralism from the Perspective of Interculturation" in Kuncheria Pathil (ed.), *Religious Pluralism: An Indian Christian Perspective* (Delhi: ISPCK, 1991), 255-256.

[62] O. V. Jathana, "Religious Pluralism- A Theological Critique", *Bangalore Theological Forum* 31/2 (1999): 6-8.

[63] R. Panikkar, "The Jordan, The Tiber and The Ganges: Three Kairological Moments of Christic Self Consciousness" in John Hick and Paul F. Knitter (eds.), *The Myth of Christian Uniqueness: Towards a Pluralistic Theology of Religions* (New York: Orbis Book, 1988), 109-110.

[64] O. V. Jathana, "Religious Pluralism- A Theological Critique", 16.

[65] Dank freed Reetz, "R. Panikkar's Theology of Religions", *Religion and Society* XV/3 (September- 1968): 32.

Panikkar's theology of religions is a transforming syncretism or as a religious hybridity.[66]

1.6.2 Dialogue

For Panikkar Dialogue is the means for the ultimate goal. Dialogue is neither debate nor comparative religion, but it is primarily a religious task: meeting God in one's neighbor. Panikkar proposes intra religious dialogue which means "an inner dialogue within me, an encounter in the depth of my personal religiousness, having met another religious experience on that very intimate level...[67] In the intra religious dialogue one speaks to oneself, questioning one's own religious beliefs, attitudes and practices.[68] For Panikkar dialogue is the way to overcome solipsism and egoisms of every kind.[69] Panikkar is against epoch in dialogue, particularly phenomenological epoch (introductory knowledge of a particular religiousness).

Panikkar concurs that ...I bracket my personal faith because faith I do not want to impose it on my partner nor to influence him (sic) in the least regarding the contents of our dialogue... Meet him (sic) on his (sic) own ground, having renounced my personal standing.[70] He has characterized his personal attitude as to accept the risk of conversion without alienation, assumption without repudiation, synthesis without syncretism or eclecticism.[71] He continues to argue "I am proposing either a facile eclectic spot for the spiritual picnic of shallow spiritualities. I am proposing a Temple of understanding, a Mosque of Reconciliation, a church of Love, a Gurudwara of peace,

---

[66] Amos Young, *Hospitality and the Other: Pentecost, Christian Practices and the Neighbor* (New York: Orbis Book, 2008), 90.

[67] R. Panikkar, *Intra-Religious Dialogue* (Bangalore: ATC, 1984), 78.

[68] Anto Karokaran, "Raimond Panikkar's Theology of Religion: A Critique", 22.

[69] R. Panikkar, "The Encounter of Religions: The Unavoidable Dialogue", 167.

[70] R. Panikkar, "The Internal Dialogue- The Insufficiency of the So-called Phenomenological Epoch in the Religious Encounter", *Religion and Society* 15/3 (September-1968): 57.

[71] Dominic Veliath, "From Ontonomy to Dialogical Dialogue: A Passacoglia", 194. Cited from R. Panikkar, "Philosophy as Life Style" in A. Mercier and M. Svilar (eds.), *Philosophers on their Own Works* Vol: 4 (Frankfurt: Lasvegues, (1978): 200-201.

a Gompa of Compassion, a Stupa of Reverence, a Forest of joy, a Tree of Insight, a House of Fire and especially a hall for the Word."[72] That is why he speaks of ecumenical ecumenism.

1.6.2.1 Ecumenical Ecumenism

It is an ecumenism among world religions same as ecumenism among Christians. According to Paul Knitter, Panikkar's ecumenical ecumenism strives for unity without harming diversity.[73] Here, he discerns common origin and goal or mystery in all religions. That is what he calls the *fundamental religious fact.* The purpose of this ecumenism is to deepen one's grasp and living of this mystery. In order to happen this, Panikkar insists that the traditional religions must give up any pretense to monopoly of what religion stands for.[74] The great temptation for ecumenism is to extrapolate- to use a native growth beyond the bonds of its native soil.[75]

1.6.3 Church and Christianity

1.6.3.1 Church

Panikkar makes the distinction between church and Christianity. Church is nor a religion[76] but *ecclesia* strictly speaking, implies an organism, not an organization. An organism needs a soul, life. An organization requires an idea, a rationale.[77] Church, therefore, doesn't admit religious discrimination-that the religions do not infer a fundamental discrimination between man (sic) and man (sic): that goodness and evil, truth and error, salvation and damnation…[78] His

---

[72] R. Panikkar, "A Religious Meditation on Ayodhya", *Journal of Dharma* 25/1 (January-March: 2000): 21.

[73] Paul F. Knitter, *No Other Name* (Philippines: Claretian Publications, n.d), 153.

[74] R. Panikkar, "Have Religions the Monopoly on Religion", *Journal of Ecumenical Studies* 11 (1974): 16.

[75] R. Panikkar, *Intra-Religious Dialogue,* 41.

[76] Dominic Veliath, "Christ and Religious Pluralism- Raimundo Panikkar", *Jeevadhara* 28/165 (May- 1998): 217.

[77] R. Panikkar, "Christendom, Christianity, Christianness", *Jeevadhara* 21/124 (July-1991): 324.

[78] R. Panikkar, "Church and World Religions", *Religion and Society* 14/2 (June-1967): 60.

vision of church can be understood as follows: "church should learn from Hinduism in such a way that ecclesial consciousness does not need to be a *closed group consciousness* and that self-identify does not need to be affirmed against the background of different identity.[79] Therefore, church might as well try to develop a catholic universal consciousness in today's real global context.

1.6.3.2 Christianity

Initially there was an accent on the superiority of Christianity over against other religions. So, he argues that Christianity is the end, the fulfillment of religions. Later on he says that the word Christian can be adjectival content of Christendom (a civilization), of Christianity (a religion), and of Christianness (personal religiousness).[80] Christian is the member of the Christendom belongs to the past and the future. When Christendom began to collapse in the 16th century it was replaced by the Christianity as a religion. For Panikkar Christiannss is confessing a personal faith, adopting a Christ like attitude in as much as Christ represents the central symbol of one's own life.[81] In short, Christianity and church cannot have, as a religion, any uniqueness, superior function, absolute claim of truth, university, etc. by virtue of a historical revelation.

1.6.4 Christology

Christology is one of the greatest contributions of Panikkar to humanity is his insight in to the mystery of Christ. The climax of Panikkar's Christological formulation, a Advaitic Christology is expressed in his noted work. *The Unknown Christ of Hinduism* wherein he interprets Brahma Sutra 1:1, 2. He interprets this text as follows "that from which this world comes forth and to which it returns and by which it is sustained that that is Christ.[82] He goes on to argue that Christ is already there in Hinduism in so far as Hinduism

---

[79] R. Panikkar, "Hindu Ecclesial Consciousness- Some Ecclesiological Reflection", *Jeevadhara* 21 (May-June: 1974): 203.

[80] R. Panikkar, "Christendom, Christianity, Christianness, 324.

[81] *Ibid.,* 326.

[82] R. Panikkar, *The Unknown Christ of Hinduism* (London: Darton, Longman, Todd, 1964), 131.

is a true religion; Christ is already at work in any Hindu prayer as far it is really payer...[83] Panikkar's Christological formulation in the light of Advaita Vedanta is a super structure built on various assumptions such as the context of Christology, the universal ontic Christ, Christ as a mediator and savior and the transformation of Christology into Christophany.

1.6.4.1 Ontic Christology

In Christology Panikkar highlights the universal saviorhood of Christ to His cosmic action and presence in all relation and being rather than action and presence in Jesus of Nazareth.[84] In this understanding he also makes distinction between the Universal *Christ and Particular Jesus.* He affirms that Christ is the savior is not to be restricted to the merely historical figure of Jesus of Nazareth. He, therefore, concludes that Jesus is historical name (finite) Christ is the name above every name (infinite). Christians therefore should acknowledge that all religions recognize in one way or another this Christ, the name above all names-Christ- can go by many historical names: Rama, Krishna, Isvara, Purusha, Tathangatha so forth and so on.[85] Christ is one of the multiple manifestations of the infinite or the sacred.[86] According to Panikkar Christ is to be seen not only in the limited Abrahamistic or Semitic tradition but also in the cosmic tradition of humankind and in all authentic religious traditions.[87] Thus, Panikkar links Christology to Christophany.

1.6.4.2 Christophany

For him the word Christophany, unlike Christology suggests that the encounter with Christ cannot be reduced to a simple doctrinal or intellectual approach... allows not only better understanding of

---

[83] *Ibid.,* 17.

[84] R. Panikkar, "Neither Christo-monism nor Christo-dualism", *Jeevadhara* 14/142 (July-1994): 337.

[85] R. Panikkar, *Trinity and Religious Experience of Man,* 53-54.

[86] Sebastian Karotenprel, "Inter-Religious Dialogue" in Roger E. Hedlund and Paul Joshua Bhakiaraj (eds.), *Missiology for the 21st Century* (Delhi: ISPCK, 2004), 342.

[87] Jacob Parapally, "Christophany: R Panikkar's Insight in to Mystery of Christ", *Jeevadhara* 35/207 (May-2005): 259.

other traditions, but also penetrating, more profoundly inside the mystery of Christ.[88] Panikkar's Christophany is inseparable from his Christology, if Christology is root, Christophany is the fruit. Panikkar is back with a ground breaking treatise on Christology. *The Fullness of Man: A Chrisophany*. The first part deals with the Christophanic experience- Christophany is more experiential in nature. It is experience of union. Christophanic doesn't split Christ's immanence into one part human, and the other divine: it is an Advaitic experience.[89] The second part conveys mystical experience of Jesus can be attained by any human being. For him it was pure human experience... ultimately experience of man (sic) as man (sic).[90]

In the final part Panikkar describes Christophany in nine theses or sutras: ***firstly,*** Christ is the symbol of all reality-because in him are enclosed not only all treasures of divinity but also all mysteries of man (sic) and all density of the universe.[91] ***Secondly,*** a Christian knows Christ in and through Jesus- in and trough Christian revelation and experience not a mere confession. ***Thirdly,*** Christ's identity is not his identification- Christophany seeks to maintain the equilibrium between the identification and identity of Jesus or between the Jesus of history and the Christ of faith.[92] ***Fourthly,*** Christians do not have monopoly of the knowledge of Christ. ***Fifthly,*** Christophany is the overcoming of a tribal Christology.[93] ***Sixthly,*** Christophany considers that protological, historical and eschatological Christ is one and the same reality distended in time, extended in space and intentional in

---

[88] R. Panikkar, "Christology and Christophany", *Third Millennium* II (October-December: 1999): 10.

[89] R. Panikkar, *The Fullness of Man: A Christophany,* Trans. Dilascia Alfred (Delhi: ISPCK, 2006), 23.

[90] *Ibid.,* 138.

[91] Jacob Parapally, "Christophany: R. Panikkar's Insight into Mystery of Christ" 261. Cited from R. Panikkar, "A Christophany of Our Times", *Theology Digest* 39/1 (1992): 5.

[92] *Ibid.,* 261.

[93] It means that contemporary Christology must incorporate the insight about the mystery which Christians call Christ and which manifests itself in other religions. (See, Jacob Parapally, 262).

us. It expresses the unity of Christ as Creator, Redeemer and Glorifier. Christophany helps us to integrate past, present and future and thus live consciously a Tempiternal life.[94] ***Seventh Sutra*** says incarnation is also inculturation. For Panikkar incarnation is not only a historical event but also a cultural event intelligible in a particular cultural context. ***Eighth sutra*** conveys that Christophany reveals to us the reality of a church which has no boundaries (cosmic church). ***Finally,*** Christophany is the manifestation of the mysterious union of the divine, human and cosmic dimension of reality (cosmotheandric intuition).[95] Panikkar, therefore, concludes that in Jesus Christ the finite and infinite meet, in him the human and divine are united. In him the material and the spiritual are one to say nothing of masculine and feminine, high and low, heaven and earth and obviously the historical and transhistorical, time and eternity.[96]

1.6.5 Cosmotheandrism

Cosmotheandrism is a key concept in Panikkar. This thought emerged out of his concern for the Hindu-Christian encounter. Coining the word cosmotheandric or theanthropocosmic, Panikkar brings out the three irreducible dimension of reality: God *(Theos)*, human *(Anthropos)* and nature *(Cosmos)*. He also finds inseparability (interrelatedness) and distinction between them (inter-independence). Panikkar understands its variation in different degrees and diverse ways: in some things divine may be more prominent (creation), in others the human may shine forth brightly (in Gandhi) and in still others the cosmic may appear more striking (like in the stability and solidarity of some things).[97] In his understanding of Cosmotheandrism, there is a kind of *perichoresis,* 'dwelling within one another' of these three dimensions of reality, the divine, the human and the cosmic-the I,

[94] Jacob Parapally, "Christophany: R. Panikkar's Insight in to Mystery of Christ", 262.

[95] *Ibid.,* 263.

[96] *Ibid.* Cited from R. Panikkar, "A Christophany of Our Times", 20.

[97] Francis X. D'sa, "The Interreligious Dialogue of the Future: Exploration into the Cosmotheandric Nature of Dialogue", *VJTR* 61/10 (October-1997): 701.

the you and the it.[98] Cosmotheandric experience is a mystical and is deeply personal while at the same time being universal and inter-relational.[99]

1.6.5.1 Cosmotheandric Intuition

According to Panikkar cosmotheandric intuition is the emerging religious consciousness of our times. Modern man (sic) has killed an isolated and insular God; the contemporary earth is killing a merciless and rapacious man (sic) and the gods often seem to have deserted both man (sic) and cosmos.[100] Panikkar elucidated his understanding of each of these dimensions. Panikkar considers cosmic dimension as the body dimension of reality which is tangible, concrete and objectifiable. So, Panikkar states a metaphysical truth- whatever this may be is only true if it is really *Kataphysical.*[101] Panikkar discerns divine dimension as totally other. He expounds divine dimension as the "infinite inexhaustibility of any human being, its ever open character, its mystery- if we allow the word in this connection, its freedom, and another language might prefer.[102] Panikkar describes human dimension in terms of consciousness-everything is living and conscious as the humans. Panikkar strikes at the basis of human and his consciousness which is sectored into non-historical, historical and transhistorical- The tripod of conciousness.[103] Cosmotheandrism, in short, represents an effort and a vision where there is a happy

[98] L. Anthoni Savari Raj, "The End of Reality: Raimon Panikkar's Cosmotheandric Vision and Its Implications", *JICPR* XXIV/ 1 (January-March: 2007): 138. Cited from R. Panikkar, "The Myth of Pluralism: The Tower of Babel-A Meditation on Non-Violence", *Cross Currents* 29 (Summer- 1979): 217.

[99] Brad Banon, "The Eco-Pneumatology of Raimon Panikkar", *Journal of Dharma* 31/4 (October-December: 2006): 467.

[100] R. Panikkar, "Cosmotheandric Intuition", *Jeevadhara* 14/79 (January-1984): 35.

[101] L. Anthoni Savari Raj, "The End of Reality: Raimon Panikkar's Cosmotheandric Vision and Its Implications", 139. Cited from R. Panikkar, "Colligite Fragmenta", Elgo F. A. and Fittipaldi S. E. (eds.), *From Alienation to at Oneness* (Villanova: n.p, 1977), 78.

[102] *Ibid.*

[103] Ashwanth Amalraj, "The Cosmotheandric Vision of Ecology: A Philosophical Enterprise", *Jnanodaya* 16 (June-2009): 120.

marriage between the secular and the scared, which Panikkar calls as *sacred secularity.*[104] This tripod relation is further explained in his theology of trinity.

1.6.5.2 Ecosophy

It is Panikkar who coined this term to the world of theology. Eco is derived from the Greek *oikos,* meaning house. Sophy comes from the Greek Sophia, meaning wisdom. It carries two meanings; in the one sense, it is the wisdom that we have about the earth. Panikkar however employs another meaning of the term- Ecosophy is the wisdom of the earth.[105] If ecology is an active discipline of study and involvement in nature, Ecosophy is a passive discipline of listening to nature and recognizing that we are always already involved in nature. He criticizes the human attitude towards earth. For him "earth is the fertile womb of life but not its source. She is the womb of beings. She receives the seed of the divine and transforms it into abundant life. The earth is where and how-the divine manifests its bounty and its power to man (sic).[106]

1.7 Panikkar: A Pilgrimage

Undoubtedly one can say that Panikkar is truly a pilgrimage to contemporary theological consciousness. For, he is an itinerary in his thought and theological process. There are at least three areas wherein Panikkar can be considered to be a pilgrimage. At the *mystical* level in which he was attempting to relate to one another in a pluralistic world. Both Unknown Christ of Hinduism and Intra-Religious Dialogue reveal the profound stirrings of an existential conversation percolating deep within the soul of a cosmopolitan mystic.[107] At the *philosophical level,* he is a lover of wisdom. This level is revealed in his notion of Cosmotheandrism. Finally, at the *theological level,* Panikkar's project emerges Vis-a-Vis the Christian theological

---

[104] R. Panikkar, *Worship and Secular Man,* 9.

[105] Brad Banon, "The Eco-Pneumatology of Raimon Panikkar", 458.

[106] R. Panikkar, *The Cosmotheandric Experience: Emerging Religious Consciousness* (Delhi: Motilal Banarsidass, 1998), 138.

[107] Amos Young, *Hospitality and the Other: Pentecost, Christian Practices and the Neighbor,* 91.

tradition and his proposal of metatheology as fundamental theology proves this very fact. According to him fundamental theology is a pre-theological or philosophical reflection on the foundations of theology. He goes on to argue that fundamental theology becomes rather a kind of diacritical theology… on the message of different religions.[108] At this juncture he relates Christian theology to that of Sankara's Vedanta and thus he deserves criticism. In short, Panikkar is mystically a monk, philosophically a lover and theologically an arbitrator. So, he always revolves around these three levels and looks for a synthesis.

Conclusion

Raimundo Panikkar is truly a gifted linguist. More often than not, his theology and philosophy resemble poetry more than prose. Unfortunately, this tends to make his writings quite challenging for readers who are not at least somewhat familiar with Greek, Latin and Sanskrit languages and literatures. As it is explained above Panikkar's basic theology emerged from his multicultural heritage and therefore, the entire theological thought and journey are the reflection of his conviction of the recognition of Christ in other religions, particularly Hinduism. Felix Wilfred Observes that Panikkar's theological vision is rather something like the coat of Joseph-made of many colors.[109] All these thoughts of Panikkar reveal the fact that he is more inclined to Hinduism. Arguably, Amos Young characterized Panikkar to be a hybridized religious thinker.[110] However, Panikkar's Advaitic theology and his theological approach in philosophical orientation invites critical appraisal. This philosophical orientation is very much highlighted in the doctrine of Trinity.

---

[108] R. Panikkar, "Meta theology or Diacritical theology is Fundamental Theology", *Concilium 6/5* (June-1969): 21.

[109] Felix Wilfred, *Beyond Settled Foundations: The Journey of Indian Theology* (Madras: University of Madras, 1993), 100.

[110] Amos Young, *Hospitality and the Other: Pentecost, Christian Practices and the Neighbor,* 90.

Chapter 2

Trinity and Hindu Spirituality
Panikkar's Triadic Synthesis

2.0 Introduction

Throughout the centuries Christian theologians have been simultaneously perplexed and inspired by the doctrine of trinity. Countless philosophical attempts have tried to balance the trinity. One among them was Raimon Panikkar who introduced advaitan color to trinity to the theological world. Similar view is highlighted in his books *The Trinity and World Religious* (1970), its revised edition named *The Trinity and the Religious Experience of Man* (1973) and an essay entitled *The Jordan, The Tiber and The Ganges.* The pioneers of Indian ashram movement, as we see, have great liking for *Sat-Cit-Ananda* as the Indian expression of trinity. Panikkar studiously avoids this terminology and finds his clue in the traditional types of spiritualities or *margas* of Hinduism: *Karma, Bhakti and Jnana.* In recent debates on religious pluralism, the theology of trinity has gained more prominence. As he expounds trinity in terms of Hindu spirituality this chapter briefly explain Hindu Spirituality in general and his understanding on trinity in particular.

2.1. Hindu Spirituality

2.1.1 Definition

According to Margaret Chatterjee Indian language have no word either for religion or for spirituality.[111] Yet, the Indian word *sadhana* share a common characteristic with the term spirituality. Traditionally, *sadhana* means creation harmony between spirituality and Worldly life. Gordon S. Wakefield defines spirituality as a world which describes those attitudes, beliefs; practices which animate people's lives and help them reach out towards super sensible realities.[112] Gandhi considered his work as a *sadhana* and Tagore interpreted *sadhana* in terms of artistic experience.[113]

It is precisely in *sadhana* that they differ and they differ essentially and basically. For *Mahabharatha* describes various *vratas* (vows) practiced by different kinds of *Sadhakas*[114]... *but* Upanishads contain different *vidhyas* is apt to demonstrate the immense variety of *sadhanas.*[115] It is therefore, not speak of Indian spirituality as such. Contrastingly, Panikkar prefers Hindu Spirituality which necessitates re-interpretation in Indian Christian theology, for Hindu spirituality is applied only to high castes.

2.1.1.1 Christian Interpretation

The substantive 'spirituality' does not occur in the scripture, but the adjective 'spiritual' is frequently employed to describe a character of a man (sic) who has entered into the Kingdom of God.[116] Elizabeth defines spirituality is an outward journey into the world transcending

---

[111] Margaret Chatterjee, *The Concept of Spirituality* (New Delhi; Allied Publishers, 1989), 19.

[112] Gordon S. Wakefield, "Spirituality" in G. S. Wakefield (ed.), *The Dictionary of Christian Spirituality (*London: SCM Press, 1983), 361.

[113] Klaus Klostermaier, 'Sadhana-Sketch of Indian Spirituality", *Religion and Society,* XVI/2 (June-1969); 338. Cited from, Gandhi's Autobiography and Tagore's Sadhana.

[114] One who practices *sadhana.*

[115] Klaus Klostermaier, "Sadhana-Sketch of Indian Spirituality", 38.

[116] David Fyffe, "Spirituality" in James Hastings (ed.), *Encyclopedia of Religion and Ethics,* Vol. 11 (Edinburgh: T & T Clark, 1974), 808.

the spirituality and material dichotomy.[117] Another viable and meaningful definition is, spirituality may be described as the manner in which a person views his relation with God, other persons and the world in general, and response to this relation in so far as it enriches, enables and elevates him (sic) fulfilling his (sic) desire for inner peace, total realization and ultimate happiness.[118] Spirituality also proposes a set of practices *(sadhana)* coming from an underlying theory-adopted more or less spontaneously by some people which lead them to perfection.[119]

Christian spirituality is neither abstract knowledge nor mere moralism. It is not a human system of self perfection, even in the moral or religious order, nor a program of psychological conditioning to induce certain states of soul.[120] Hence, the relation of Christian spirituality to that of other religions is a matter which is likely to loom ever larger… and seem to suffer from an embarrassment of riches; confused syncretism and retreat into pietistic and bigoted sentimentality are both to be deplored.[121] Hinduism really lacks this vision of spirituality, for spirituality that tries to ignore the realities of life, cannot be called spirituality. According to Mathew Vekathanam spirituality may be understood as man's (sic) existence.[122] Outsider views Hindu spirituality as incomprehensive and unharmonious on account of two observations; spirituality in Hindu thought is ceremonial and external on the one hand, and mystical and subjective on the other and in the life of a Hindu, spirituality may take the

---

[117] Elizabeth, "Liberative Spirituality and Feminist Models of Ecclesia as Resource for a Dalit model of the Church", *NCCR,* CXVIII/6 (June-July: 1998): 401.

[118] Antony Edanad, "Interiorized Word and Transforming Spirit: Johannine Model of Spirituality", *Journal of Dharma,* XIII/3 (July-September: 1988): 238.

[119] Indian Theological Association 14th Annual Meeting, "Towards an Indian Christian Spirituality in a Pluralistic Context", *VJTR,* 55/3 (March-1991): 164.

[120] E. E. Larkin, 'Christian Spirituality" in William J. McDonald (ed.), *New Catholic Encyclopedia* (London/Sydney: McGrow Hill Book Co., 1967), 599.

[121] Gordon S. Wakefield, "Spirituality", 363.

[122] Mathew Vekathanam, "Mystery, Myth, History: Dimensions of Spirituality in the Context of Advaita", *Journal of Dharma* XIII/3 (July-September: 1998): 204.

form of sanctifying or deifying a rock, a tree, an animal and a man (sic).[123]

2.1.2 Development

Hindu spirituality has been developed in three different stages: in the *Vedic period* Aryans believed that sacrificial karmas would take them to heaven (Karma Marga); in the *Upanishads* importance is stressed on meditation and the observation of the laws. Meditation is focused upon the fact that *Brahman* alone is real. This is called *Jnana Marga* or the way of knowledge. In spite of the synthetic nature of the *Bhagavat Gita,* the emphasis on the grace of God and devotion of God created *Bhakti Marga* or the way of devotion.[124]

2.1.3 Foundations

To study Hindu Spirituality one needs to be strongly rooted in the four basic concepts of Hinduism- Reality, World, Human life and Self/ Soul because there is a continuity of divinity in them.

2.1.3.1 Reality

Though there are different opinions regarding reality, Hinduism embodies very definite and catholic convictions about reality or god. This can be understood by clarifying three major questions about reality in Hinduism. ***Firstly,*** whether reality is one or many? People of other faiths opined that Hindus worship many gods. A reasonable Hindu would find it unfounded. Of course, all serious Hindu thinkers and followers of Hinduism have affirmed with one accord that reality is one.[125] The famous *Rig Vedic* declaration is that reality is one but sages call it by various names such an all inclusive and catholic understanding of Hindu concept of reality is quite conducive to the pluralistic context of India where varied forms of understanding of reality abound. ***Secondly,*** whether reality has any attribute? Of course, a majority of Hindu forms of worship are patterned after the popular

---

[123] George A. Mather and Larry A. Nichols, (eds.), *Dictionary of Cult, Sects, Religions and the Occults* (Edinburgh: T & T Clark, 1993), 760.

[124] S. Robertson, "Hindu Spirituality", *Religion and Society,* 50/2 (June-2005): 18.

[125] *Ibid.,* 2.

and prevalent notion that god posses qualities. ***Thirdly,*** whether god is transcendent or immanent? The predominant accepted answer is god is both. According to Radhakrishnan God is neither completely transcendent nor completely immanent.[126] It underlines the fact that the one Ultimate Reality is dwelling in the human beings or human being is divine, is the focal point of Hindu spirituality.

2.1.3.2 World

There are innumerable interpretations about the world: For Sankara the world is *Maya,* Ramanuja explained that the world is dependent on God, Vallabhas and Chaitanya hold that God is the material and efficient cause of the world and according to Tantra, it has neither a beginning nor an end.[127] They view that world is divine or spiritual entity.

2.1.3.3 Human Life

Hinduism recognizes that human beings are divine because God is living in them.[128] In short, it looks upon man (sic) as a spiritual being.[129] S. P. Dubey observes that Indians have taken, in general the realization of spiritual reality to be goal of life.[130]

2.1.3.4 Self or Soul

Every Hindu believes that the soul to be eternal. But the troubling question is whether there is one soul or many? Except Sankara all would affirm that it is wrong to identity the self with the body or to say that there is only one self in all bodies, for there are as many selves as there are bodies.[131] Another common conviction of Hindus is that the soul is in bondage which means *Samsara* (cycle of births and

---

[126] S. Radhakrishnan, *An Idealist View of Life,* 2nd Edition (London: George Allen and Unwin, 1951), 106.

[127] Satish Chandra Chatterjee, "Hindu Religious Thought" Kenneth Morgan (ed.) *The Religion of Hindus* (Delhi: Motilal Banarsidass, 1986), 249.

[128] S. Robertson, "Hindu Spirituality", 5.

[129] P. Nagaraja Rao, "A Contemporary Hindu Understanding of Salvation", *Bangalore Theological Forum,* 5/2 (July-December 1973): 37.

[130] S. P. Dubey, 'The Indian View of Life", *NCCR,* CIII/9 (September-1983): 425.

[131] Satish Chandra Chatterjee, "Hindu Religion Thought', 235.

deaths).[132] The starting point of Hindu spirituality therefore is, the realization that the souls are eternal, they suffer *samsara* on account of their ignorance and salvation or liberation of the soul.

2.2 Hindu Spirituality as Margas

It is said that main purpose of life is union with God, to accomplish this ordinarily three margas are being taught; Karma, Bhakti and Jnana.

2.2.1 Karma Marga

The very word has a good pedigree in India literature, but its meaning is complex and needs the context to determine it. The root of the word is *kr* meaning to act, to do in the noblest sense of the word.[133] Traditionally, karma is understood as the sacrificial activity (ritual activity) of human beings while in the *Sramanic Culture*[134] it became more personal and ethical-person's actions as determining his or her future existence.[135] At the same time karma marga neither means freewill, nor fatalism but determination of the present by the past.[136] Bhagavat Gita talks about both karma and dharma. Former is a law of cause and effect and latter is largely ethical and religious. *Nishkama Karma* is the overarching concept in Bhagavat Gita which is translated as desireless action, selfless action, duty for duty sake, work done without attachment nor expecting the fruits there of.[137]

---

[132] S. Robertson, "Hindu Spirituality', 7.

[133] G. Gispert Sauch, 'Karma" in G. Gispert Sauch (ed.), *Gems from India* (Delhi: ISPCK, 2006), 88.

[134] Culture based on sramanas which is one the divisions of Vedas.

[135] G. Gispert Sauch, "Karma", 89.

[136] Joachim Werner, "Karma marga in the Ramayana", *Gurukul Journal of Theological Studies*, 7/1, 2 (1996-97): 96.

[137] Anthony Kolenchery, "Nishkama Karma- An Indian Paradigm for New Social Order', *Indian Theological Studies*, XXXVI/1 (March-1999): 6.

2.2.2 Bhakti Marga

The word Bhakti derived from the root *bhaj* and that signifies love. Hence, Bhakti marga is the marga of deep love for God.[138] Swamy Narendranand goes on to argue that love is manifested not in flowery words but in unfeigned acts.[139] Bhakti simply means religious devotion or piety as a means of salvation. In the Sanskrit literature the term Bhakti has a wide meaning, implying the relationship between men, between men and women and between God and human beings.[140] Philosophers interpreted it very precisely for instance, Madhava defines it as firm and unshakable love of God, which rises above all other ties of love and affection based upon an adequate knowledge and conviction of his great majesty is called Bhakti.[141] Gispert Sauch observes that Bhakti is both as antithesis and a complement of Advaita, for it teaches a personal relation of love with God.[142]

2.2.3 Jnana Marga

Jnana has great depths of meaning the noun occurs more than 60 times in the Bhagavat Gita and the verb around 25 times, not counting equivalent expressions. The *Upanishads-* the *Janakanda* of the Vedas are the basic text for it, it is the state of enlightenment which is possible only through knowledge. The basic tenet of Jnana marga, therefore is, liberation comes only from knowledge. It is said that *Sadhaka* has to transcend the world of waking-consciousness, of dream and dreamless sleep in order to realize in *Turiya,* the nature of the Absolute. The *Mahavakyas* express the final insight for it; *Aham brahmasmi* (I am Brahman). *Aham atman Brahman,* etc.[143]

Considering these margas as framework Panikkar expounds his theory of trinity and builds a 'triple schema', relating them to the

---

[138] Swamy Narendranand, *Hindu Spirituality* (Sultampur, UP: Jyoti Ashram, n.d), 2.

[139] *Ibid.*

[140] W. M. Callewaert, "God in Early Hindi Bhakti: Male and Female", *Journal of Dharma,* 5/2 (April-June 1980): 197.

[141] Klaus Klostermaier, "Sadhana; A Sketch of Indian Spirituality", 46. Cited from, Madhava, *Mahabharata Tatparya Nirnaya I,* 86.

[142] G. Gispert Sauch, "Bhakti" in G. Gispert Sauch (ed.), *Gems From India,* 93.

[143] Klaus Klostermaier, "Sadhana: A Sketch of Indian Spirituality", 47.

special spirituality of Father (Karma Marga), the Son (Bhakti Marga) and the Spirit (Jnana Marga).[144] Ewert Cousins points out "Panikkar's this innovative approach is in keeping with the well established universalizing tendency in the tradition of Christian theology."[145]

2.3 Panikkarian Trinity

2.3.1 Indian Theological Understanding

Till the emergence of Indian Christian theology doctrine of trinity has been examined through the medium of western languages-Greek. Latin and English. Later trinity is expressed not only in Indian terms but through Indian ways of thought.[146] There are three ways in which Indian theologians interpreted the trinity: in term of *Sat-Cit-Anada* (K.C. Sen, B. Upadhyaya, Jules Monchanin and Swamy Abhishiktananda), in terms of *Bhakti Marga* (Manilal Parekh) and in terms of *Hindu Spirituality* (Panikkar). Why Panikkar is distinct from other theologians is authentically explained by Panikkar himself; one religion in fact may include several spiritualities, because spirituality is not directly bound up with any dogma or institution. It is rather an attitude of mind which one may ascribe to different religions.[147]

2.3.2 Basic Pre-Suppositions

He begins his treatment of the trinity by stating that 'my intention here is not to expound the doctrine of trinity; my desire is simply to show in the light of the trinity three forms of spirituality described above can be *reconciled.*[148]

For him trinity is ultimate *foundation* for pluralism and he underlines the significance of this approach for the encounter of religions. Panikkar, therefore, affirms that trinity then may be

---

[144] A. M. Mundadan, "Hindu Christian Dialogue", *Jeevadhara,* XI/65 (1981): 387.

[145] E. H. Cousins, "Trinity and the World Religions", *Journal of Ecumenical Studies,* 7 (1970): 476-478.

[146] Robin Boyd, *Kristadvaita* (Madras: CLS, 1977), 410.

[147] R. Panikkar, *The Trinity and the Religious Experience of Man* (London: Orbis Books, 1973), 9.

[148] *Ibid.,* 41.

considered as a *junction* where the authentic spiritual dimensions of all religions meet.[149]

In spite of all relative statements regarding trinity, Panikkar asserts that trinity is the *foundation stone* of Christianity and the *existential basis* of Christian life.[150]

Panikkar's trinity represents one of the most profound problems that a human being can ask about God, about himself, one of the most urgent queries at the very root of the human situation and its many problems.[151]

Panikkar asserts that it is simply an unwarranted over statement to affirm that the Trinitarian conception of the ultimate and with it the whole of reality is an exclusive Christian insight or revelation.[152]

He also admitted that *Logos Christology* is not so helpful or faithful in encounter with Hinduism or Buddhism. Panikkar notes that neither *advaitan* Hinduism with its concept of the non duality of self and the Absolute nor Buddhism with its notion of *nirvana* has grounding in a concept of *Logos* nor indeed they both negate it.[153]

He considered that trinity is the fulcrum of Christian experience.[154]

The trinity, *trikaya,* the *Sat-Cit-Ananda*, the *triloka* of practically every religion, the three spatial, temporal and anthropological dimensions, etc., seem to be rooted more deeply within reality than any merely heuristic or epistemological device or scheme.[155]

So, he interprets trinity in relation to the entire web of Reality. For he understands reality as the very relationship, the radical relativity, the non dualistic ground, summit or whatever we may

---

149 *Ibid.,* 42.

150 *Ibid.*

151 Dominic Veliath, "The Trinity in Indian Theology", *Kristu Jyoti,* 8/2 (June-1992): 11.

152 Ibid., 13.

153 Anne Hunt, *Trinity* (New York: Orbis Books, 2005), 151.

154 R. Panikkar, *The Fullness of Man; A Christophany,* Trans. Alfred Di Lascia (Delhi: ISPCK, 2006), 120.

155 R. Panikkar, *The Cosmotheandric Experience: Emerging Religious Consciousness* (Delhi: Motilal Banarsidas, 1998), 55.

choose according to our system of reference.[156] Collaboration not only among religions but with modern human at large. At this juncture he renders dialogical dialogue which is not a matter of comparing religions, but a process whereby one tries to grow together... Christian commitment demands that one be ready to enter into the experience of others.[157]

2.3.3 Formative Factors

2.3.3.1 Pluriform of Religious Settings

As he was brought up within three religious traditions, he explicitly applies trinity to the three corresponding forms of spirituality in the following manner. The silent, the apophatic dimension corresponds to the Father. This apophatic spirituality Panikkar relates to the Buddhist experience of *nirvana* or *nihilism.* The personalistic dimension corresponds to the Son... This personalistic spirituality according to Panikkar is, similar to the Judeo-Christian and Islamic perspective of religiosity. The immanent dimension of spirituality relates to the Spirit, has its resonance in the Hindu Advaita or the non duality of the self and the Absolute.[158] Paul Chung rightly identified that Panikkar also makes an effort to deepen the meaning of the trinity from outside the *Logos* that is from silence of Buddhism and the unity of Hinduism.[159]

2.3.3.2 Eastern Influence

According to Ewert H. Cousins Panikkar's doctrine of trinity has affinity to Greek Fathers and to the early Franciscan School.[160] In

---

[156] R. Panikkar, "The God of Silence", *Indian Journal of Theology,* 21 (1972): 123-124.

[157] R. Panikkar, "The Dialogical Dialogue" in F. Whaling (ed.)., *The World's Religious Traditions* (Edinburgh: SCM, 1984), 208.

[158] A. M. Mundadan, *Paths of Indian Theology* (Bangalore: Dharmaram Publications, 1998), 98-99.

[159] Paul Chung, "Trinity and Asian Theology of Divine Dukkar", *Asian Journal of Theology,* 16/1 (April-2002): 134.

[160] A. M. Mundadan, *Paths of Indian Theology,* Cited from E. H. Cousins, "R. Panikkar and the Christian Systematic Theology of the Future", *Cross Currents,* 29 (1979): 147.

the *Christian Tradition.* Panikkar argues that one may find basis in Ignatius of Antioch…and the most significant point of contact may be found in the mystical writing of Pseudo-Dionysius and Meister Ekhart.[161] He, therefore, cites with approval the Greek Fathers' image of the source, the river and the ocean and goes on to give his own adaptation of it: the Father is the source of Being; the Son is Being and the Spirit is the Return of Being or the Ocean of Being.[162]

2.3.3.3 Comparative Religious Hermeneutics

In the words of Panikkar comparative religion is a useful method to begin discovering certain common structures among religions and this relationship between the different tradition of the world has unfolded a kind of common typology, which is summarized in the five Kairological moments; isolation (mutual ignorance), indifference (contempt and rivalry), condemnation (conquest others), co-existence (mutual tolerance and sincere communication) and mutual fecundation (the convergence of frontiers).[163] Very fond of last Kairological moment that is mutual fecundation. He, therefore, argues that comparative religious hermeneutics implies that there is a neutral ground, a metaphilosophy, from which to critically scrutinize different religions.[164] This vision leads him to the methodological questions.

2.3.3.4 Methodological Questions

He articulates the basic questions which are multi-voiced and multi-dimensional: How one can preserve one's own identity without falling into undifferentiated collectivity? How is it possible to be a loyal Christian owing allegiance to one particular religious tradition and at the same time true to the religious traditions of the world?

---

[161] E. H. Cousins, "Trinity and the World Religions", 478.

[162] Robin Boyd, *An Introduction to Indian Christian Theology,* Revised Edition (New Delhi: ISPCK, 2004), 300.

[163] R. Panikkar, "Hermeneutics of Comparative Religion", *Journal of Dharma,* 5/1 (January-March 1980): 38-40.

[164] *Ibid.*, 41.

How can there be no man's land in the land of man (sic)?[165] He therefore, proposes trinity wherein one can find symbolic answer which is based on the imperative frame of reference.

For him imperative philosophy is a kind of learning that is reflective, critical and provisional.[166] Panikkar defines it as follows:

It is critically aware of the contingency of its own assumptions and the unavoidable necessity of resting on still unexamined presuppositions.

It is constitutively ready to question its basic foundations if they are challenged.

It is primarily concerned with searching for the primordial ground of understanding.

It attempts to form its philosophical view of reality by systematically taking into account the universal range of man's (sic) experience in as much as this is possible in any finite situation.

It is open to dialogical dialogue with other philosophical and religious views.[167]

2.4 Triadic Synthesis of Panikkar

Panikkar considers trinity as an answer to the methodological questions and thereby he attempts to connect Buddhism with the silent, self-emptying dimension of the Father; Christianity, Judaism, Islam as the religions of the Word, with the Son, the incarnate Word; and Advaitic Hinduism with the immanent, radically inner dimension of the Spirit.[168]

2.4.1 Primary Synthesis

Karma Marga for him is more similar to the iconolatry thereby he understands primary and primordial attitude of man (sic) in front of trinity. He bases his arguments on image of God of human being in which human has given himself/herself or has had implanted within

---

165 R. Panikkar, *Salvation in Christ: Concreteness and Universality, The Super Name (*California: Santa Barbara, 1972), 3.

166 R. Panikkar, "Hermeneutics of Comparative Religion", 45.

167 *Ibid.,* 45-46.

168 Mathew Illathuparampil, (ed.), *The Contemporary Theologians: Context and Contributions* (Bangalore: ATC, 2006), 365.

him (sic) an idea of the divinity as being in his (sic) own image and likeness is indubitable.[169] Subsequently, Israel also had an idol which Panikkar concurs that the idol of Israel was not an object made by hand or created by thought, an invention or discovery of man (sic); it was YHWH the living and true God who had revealed Himself to Israel and made a pact with her; who was Israel's own special idol.[170] In this sense iconolatry represents a normal dimension of the religious life of human and even the manifestation of God to human beings. Panikkar observes that iconolatry is in fact *Cosmoanthromorphism,* the attribution to God of creaturely forms, whether supra-human or sub-human.[171] If God were totally other there would be no place for love, knowledge, prayer, worship, but human spends time before their idol and submits themselves to their devoted. In short, karma marga is described as the spirituality of the Father (the one whom no human can see), because human cannot see the absolute, human tends to make images or icons of him, as do the followers of the karma marga of Hinduism. Such icons are not necessarily visible images, they may be mental and Panikkar doesn't reject them provided only they point beyond themselves.[172]

The Father is the apophatic dimension of the real. The Father has no being, the Son is his being. The Father is Absolute who has no name, no plurality, no multiplicity and no addition, so nothing could be equal or unequal. In Christian tradition this absolute has definite designation-Father/God. For him god is silence; total and absolute, the silence of being. His word who completely consumes him is the Son; the action which perfectly expresses Him is the Spirit.[173] He explains the Father in terms of the apophatism which does not mean merely that we cannot speak of the Father; most especially it means the silence of being.[174] Panikkar concludes that if we do not make image or idol of the Father we break with the Father/ Infinite.

---

[169] R. Panikkar, *The Trinity and World Religions: Icon, Person, Mystery* (Madras: CLS, 1970), 11.

[170] *Ibid.,* 12.

[171] *Ibid., 15.*

[172] Robin Boyd, *An Introduction to Indian Christian Theology,* Revised Edition, 298.

[173] R. Panikkar, *The Trinity and World Religions: Icon, Person, Mystery,* 47.

[174] R. Panikkar, *The Trinity and the Religious Experience of Man,* 47-48.

He goes on to say that the sin against the Father is the break with the infinite, the denial of our divinization...[175] The Son is the one who unveiled the image of Father, which he explains in the Bhakti marga.

2.4.2 Secondary Synthesis

Bhakti marga emphasizes religious personalism- love is no longer irrational passion or unconscious ecstasy but a mutual giving. Worship is no longer annihilation of the self before the Absolute but the voluntarily affirmation of the sovereignty. Sin is no longer cosmic transgression but refusal to love and so on.[176] Love of God necessarily demands meeting of the person, a mutual acceptance and communication between persons.[177] Son, Panikkar says, is God-from God and Light from Light.[178] For whatever is asserted of God is really asserted of the Son. He goes on to argue that Son is the Being of God...strictly speaking one does not see the Son outside the Father nor the Father outside the Son.[179] There is an interdependence and mutual penetration *(perichoresis)* between Father, Son and Spirit where the irreducible uniqueness of each person is preserved without in any way diluting their interdependence. In other words, there is an Advaitic relationship between the three persons. Father, Son and Spirit are each unique but fully interdependent so that no one can be without the other.[180]

For him Son is the "unique link between the created and the uncreated; the relative and absolute, the temporal and the eternal, earth and heaven.[181] Thus, Christ is the link or conveyer or *Pontifex Maximus (Supreme Bridge)* between these two poles, whom other religions call Isvara, Tathagatha, YHWH and Allah and so

[175] R. Panikkar, *The Trinity and World Religions: Icon, Person, Mystery,* 50.

[176] *Ibid.,* 21.

[177] Robin Boyd, *An Introduction to Indian Christian Theology,* 299.

[178] R. Panikkar, *The Trinity and World Religions: Icon, Person, Mystery,* 51.

[179] *Ibid.,* 49.

[180] Franics X. D'Sa, "The Advaitic Principle of Raimon Panikkar and Trinity" in Patrick Gnanaprakasam and Elizabeth S. Fiorenza (eds.), *Negotiating Borders: Theological Exploration in the Global Era* (Delhi: ISPCK, 2008), 165.

[181] R. Panikkar, *The Trinity and World Religions: Icon, Person, Mystery,* 52.

on.[182] Panikkar observes that His mediatorship is not primarily epistemological but ontological and thus it is ultimately not necessary to see him, provided we see through him...[183] For Panikkar, "Christ is not the revelation, not the revealed name, but the revealer of the name."[184] He concludes that Son/Christ represents both the *theosis* (divinization of human being) and *kenosis* (humanization of God).

2.4.3 Tertiary Synthesis

The spirituality of the Spirit is linked with the Upanishadic understanding of God is spirit. According to Panikkar Spirit essentially signifies the ultimate inner-ness of every being, the final foundation, the ground of being as well as beings.[185] Since, Upanishads distinguish God between the concepts of God-Immanent and God-Transcendent, Panikkar regards Spirit as God-Immanent not God-Transcendent (Absolute). The Spirit is the communion between the Father and the Son. Panikkar says in the generation of the Son, Father made an effort to empty Himself, so there no longer exists anything but nothing or nothingness, but Spirit as it were the return to the source that he himself Father. The *self* of the Father is the Son, His *in-himself* is the Spirit. Therefore, there is no room for egoism in the trinity.[186]

2.5 Trinity or Theandrism

The trinity is neither modalistic nor tri-substantial. Former attempts to explain Trinitarian mystery with the idea of being, if in fact there is a single God there can only be a single being and since in that case the three persons cannot be three beings, but a being that shares self in three perspectives internal to its very being.[187] Latter considers that there are not three substances but three persons. For Panikkar,

---

[182] *Ibid.*, 54.

[183] R. Panikkar, "The Meaning of Christ's Name in the Universal Economy of Salvation" in Joseph Pathrapankal (ed.), *Service and Salvation* (Bangalore: TPI, 1973), 262.

[184] *Ibid.*

[185] R. Panikkar, *The Trinity and World Religions: Icon, Person, Mystery,* 59.

[186] *Ibid.*, 61.

[187] *Ibid.*, 60.

the Advaita helps to solve the intra-Trinitarian problem. If Father and Son are not two they are not one either. The Spirit both unites and distinguishing them. Paul Chung acclaims those Trinitarian persons remain in the Advaitic sense as not two.[188] However, Panikkar cites Greek theologians' image- the river who flows from the source, then the Spirit as it were the end.[189] In God there is no multiplicity and there cannot be two callings or two words but he affirms that Father is the *Source* and the Son is the *Being* and the Spirit is the *Return of the Being,* which he connects with Pauline Trinitarian formula of God- *above all,* and *in all* (cf. Eph: 4, 6).[190]

At present the new situation of crisis has emerged through the meeting of different religions/faiths. To such context Panikkar synthesizes these three spirituality with that of trinity. Panikkar understands that when a Hindu most fully experience and understands Reality, he finds that s/he is close to the Christian Trinitarian experience, while the Christians understanding of their own faith and experience can be greatly deepened by entering into the three margas of Hinduism.[191] For this synthesis Panikkar rejects the adjective Trinitarian but choosing Greek, theandric. In Panikkar's words, the trinity opens us up so that we may grasp better the ultimate constitution of the real.[192]

Panikkar prefers the term theandric to describe unity which realized pragmatically between divine and human. He prefers it because Trinitarian mystery relegated to the exclusive sphere of the divinity or temporal manifestation that is creation and incarnation.[193] He also says that Trinitarian mystery has Christian connotation and claims that God is meaningless without creature thereby speaks God as *Plus Ultra.*[194]

---

[188] Paul Chung, "Trinity and Asian Theology of Divine Dukkar", 134.

[189] R. Panikkar, *The Trinity and World Religions: Icon, Person, Mystery,* 61.

[190] *Ibid.,* 68.

[191] Robin Boyd, *An Introduction to Indian Christian Theology,* Revised Edition, 300.

[192] R. Panikkar, *The Trinity and the Religious Experience of Man,* XVI.

[193] R. Panikkar, *The Trinity and World Religions: Icon, Person, Mystery,* 71.

[194] Mathew Illathuparampil, (ed.), *The Contemporary Theologians: Context and Contributions,* 363.

The term theandrism indicates two elements of every spirituality: the human and trans-human element. It maintains a harmonious synthesis to the great extent between the tensions and polarities of life; between body and the soul, spirit and matter, masculine and feminine, action and contemplation, sacred and profane, vertical and horizontal- in a word between what one may continue to all divine and what one has been accustomed to call human.[195] Here, the difficulty arises when one enters into theology proper- upon image of human and image of God. Panikkar opines that the fundamental insight of theandrism consists in the realization that human possesses an infinite capacity which links him up to the asymptotic limit called God.[196] In other words, theandrism stresses in a paradoxical fashion, the finitude of human for s/he is tending towards God the infinite and the finitude of God, for God is the end (finis) of man (sic).[197] He uses this vision as an alternative to the Dvaitic and Advaitic visions. On the one hand it succeeds in avoiding anthropomorphism and theologism on the other and it speaks to re-establish a non-dualistic vision of these two poles of reality-human and God are neither two nor one. Negatively speaking it re-establishes equilibrium rather than unity. In short, for Panikkar, God, human and world are engaged in a unique adventure and this engagement constitutes true reality and prefers theandric synthesis because every sort of particularism in fact limits itself to one or other of these attitudes, neglecting the other two and defying their complementary and essential interconnection will lead inevitably to a rigid and unilateral spirituality.[198]

2.6 Basic Deviations

Panikkar, however, points out basic pitfalls that threaten each of these ways.

---

[195] R. Panikkar, *The Trinity and World Religions: Icon, Person, Mystery,* 71.

[196] *Ibid.,* 72.

[197] Sunand Sumithra, *Christian Theologies from an Indian Perspective* (Bangalore: TBT, 2002), 186.

[198] R. Panikkar, *The Trinity and World Religions: Icon, Person, Mystery,* 75.

2.6.1 Nihilism

The basic thirst of modern human to find out absolute in them gradually leads to the gravest question that is whether the idol is the true God and the formulas dealing with it true formulas?[199] It closely corresponds to the nihilist climate of thought in our day. God cannot be exclusively an idol nor an alibi nor simply a person, nor the other *par-excellence* nor even the Supreme.[200] Consequently, a growing number of people of undeniable intellectual and moral worth reject and deny the traditional affirmations of the religions concerning the existence and nature of God. Nihilists claim that nothingness, a complete void, is the last word in the Mystery and affirm that no one even see the Father because in the final analysis there is 'nothing' to see.[201]

2.6.2 Humanism

In the West humanism is understood as a healthy reaction against an excessive emphasis on eschatology and certain anti-natural supernaturalism.[202] The staggering affirmation of Christian belief is just that it is vitally necessary to save not only the lofty part of human, his/her soul, but the whole human including his/her body. By stressing these truths lopsidedly, however, humanism very easily loses sight of the whole, upsets the balance and tends to become sheer naturalism.[203] In short, humanist attitude, however, offers unceasing witness to the utmost dignity of human life upon earth and reminds us that personal liberty and the irresistible demand of 'thy will be done' are essential elements of all true spirituality.[204]

2.6.3 Angelism

The danger inherent in the spirituality of Jnana marga is called Angelism-most certainly is not an angel. It is a common assertion

---

199 *Ibid.*

200 *Ibid.*

201 *Ibid.*, 76.

202 *Ibid.*, 77.

203 *Ibid.*

204 *Ibid.*, 78.

that human is not pure spirit on account of his/her body and human is often considered as fallen angel and goal of their nature is to reach an angelic plane.[205] It is at this point Panikkar is more inclined to Hinduism by directing our attention again and again to the absolute. But, Panikkar concludes that theandrism is a spirituality which combines in an authentic synthesis, the three dimensions of our lives on earth as well as in heaven.[206] Ewert Cousins of the opinion that Panikkar's proposal to situate a theology of non-Christian religions in the context of the trinity sits comfortably with the tradition of the Christian thought whereby everything in creation is seen as coming from and reflecting its Trinitarian Creator, the trinity of divine persons.[207] Panikkar himself presses further: just as traditional theology speaks of a *Creatio Continua,* (Continuation of Creation) not only in the flesh but also in the acts and events of all creatures. Every being is a Christophany.[208]

Conclusion

Panikkar's theology of trinity emerges as a comprehensive reality within which to situate and make sense of human spirituality as expressed in the various patterns of religious experience. Through which he wants to show that Christianity has no monopoly on Trinitarianism and proves that the Trinitarian claims of Christianity can be enriched by the contributions of different traditions. To such an attitude of Panikkar there is on the one hand, Rowan Williams ...Panikkar does an *exceptional service* to authentic engagement between traditions in their particularity, in a way not be found among pragmatic relativists.[209] On the other hand some would reject this Trinitarian approach as yet another form of *Christian*

---

[205] R. Panikkar, *The Trinity and the Religious Experience of Man,* 80.

[206] *Ibid.,* 80.

[207] Anne Hunt, *Trinity*, 156.

[208] R. Panikkar, "Jordan, the Tiber and the Ganges: Three Kairological Movements of Christic Self Consciousness" in John Hick and Paul Knitter (eds.), *The Myth of Christian Uniqueness: Towards a Pluralistic Theology of Religions* (New York: Orbis Books, 1987), 114.

[209] Rowan Williams, *On Christian Theology: Challenges in Contemporary Theology* (Malden: Blackwell, 2000), 180.

imperialism by which non-Christian religious traditions are subsumed under the Christian categories of a Trinitarian theology. What researcher would suggest is that it is not Christian imperialism but *Hindu Hegemonism* by which Christian tradition is subsumed under the Hindu categories. That is how Panikkar has viewed trinity philosophically within Hindu fold. This defect must be overcome.

Chapter 3

Influence of Hinduism on Panikkar's Theology

3.0 Introduction

In India, there has been an attempt to state the Christian faith in Indian terms and thought forms. Truly speaking, doctrine of God is one of the areas in which some theological developments have taken place. However, their approach to the problem of the nature of God has been divided along the lines of various Hindu philosophical traditions, notably Advaita. Likewise Panikkar's theology of trinity has radically been influenced by the Brahmanic tradition of Hinduism thereby his Trinitarian theology is purely Advaitic or Brahmanic. Nevertheless, Panikkar's Trinitarian theology merits a distinctively oriental and most appropriately Hindu adjective. This chapter incontrovertibly presents his understanding of Hinduism and Christianity in general and preferably, areas of influence of Hinduism on Panikkar.

3.1 Perception of Hinduism

3.1.1 Insight on Religion

According to Panikkar religion is orthopraxis and it cannot be shelved to some corners of life and to a few hours of practice; it has to permeate the whole life.[210] Meanwhile, it is evident that no religion can substitute another religion thereby the idea of a universal religion appears not to be feasible and in the given situation religions need to acknowledge one another as co-travelers towards the absolute offering, mutual support and enrichment. Hence, all religion stands in need of daily conversion *(Metanoia)*. Panikkar in this juncture opines that outdated philosophy and theology can be a hindrance to growth and therefore giving up all dogmatism and unilaterism, religion should facilitate mutual fecundation by sharing philosophical and theological insight and the mystical dimensions of religious experiences.[211] Instead, Christianity and other religions become too dogmatic as to contain all experiences under the dogmatic proclamations and affirmations thus trying to encapsulate the personal dimensions of religious experiences.[212] In this context he interprets trinity in the fold of Hindu categories.

3.1.2 Understanding of Hinduism

In the words of Panikkar the good and bonafide Hindu is saved by Christ and not by Hinduism...through the message of morality and good life... that Christ saves the Hindu morality.[213] Therefore, it is essential to understand his view of the relationship between Hinduism and Christianity.

3.1.2.1 Relationship between Hinduism and Christianity

The overarching issue in relation to Hinduism and Christianity is whether Hinduism as such has any place in the Christian economy of salvation. Panikkar adduces three groups of reasons:

---

[210] R. Panikkar, "Introduction" in Varghese Manimala *Towards Mutual Fecundation and Fulfillment of Religions,* (Delhi: Media House/ISPCK, 2009), 14.

[211] *Ibid.,* 5.

[212] R. Panikkar, *Religion y Religions* (Madrid: Editorial Gredos, 1965), 76.

[213] R. Panikkar, *The Unknown Christ of Hinduism* (London: Darton, Longman, 1964), 54.

3.1.2.1.1 Psychological and Pastoral

For Panikkar one thinks him/her self to be in full possession of the truth and believers that Christ is the carrier of God's ultimate revelation to men (sic) on earth.[214]

3.1.2.1.2 Historical Experience

This group traces out the doubt that the history of Christian nations has not been a model of righteousness and virtue, nor has the relationship between Christianity and non-Christians throughout its history been a charitable and merciful embrace.[215]

3.1.2.1.3 Theological Position

Two propositions are universally accepted by Christian theology: salvation comes exclusively through Christ and God does not condemn anybody. For Panikkar...salvation through an inner and personal act of Christ is prepared and is normally carried out by external and visible means which we call sacraments... This amount to saying that Hinduism has also a place in the universal saving providence of God.[216]

As he uses the conjunction "and" to reveal the relationship between Hinduism and Christianity, it is to say that... Hinduism comes first but that and leads it towards Christianity; our and expresses the dynamism of a transit, of a *pascha*, of a pass-over, a conversion from Hinduism to Christianity.[217] Panikkar finds inadequate those analogies which express the relationship between Hinduism and Christianity in terms of falsehood - truth, natural-supernatural.[218] Hinduism is a kind of Christianity in potency. For him Christianity is sociologically speaking...ancient paganism, or to be more precise, the complex Hebrew- Helleno- Graeco- Latino- Celtico- Gothico

---

[214] R. Panikkar, 'Hinduism and Christinity', *Religion and Society* VIII/4 (December-1961): 11.

[215] *Ibid.,* 15.

[216] *Ibid.,* 16-17.

[217] *Ibid.*

[218] Dominic Veliath, "Raimundo Panikkar- A Pilgrimage to Contemporary Ecclesiological Consciousness", *Kristu Jyoti* 5/1 (March-1989): 14.

modern religion converted to Christ with more or less success.[219] So he concludes that mission of the church cannot be indentified with one religion alone.[220]

3.1.2.2 The Most Penetrating Question

In order to understand Hinduism he ask a question, how can Hinduism come in when Christ has chosen Christianity as the place for His redeeming action?[221] For Panikkar two answers are possible: either Hinduism is excluded or Hinduism has to be included in the universal economy of salvation in Christ (as he prefers the latter). He thereby rejects any definition which sees the relationship between Hinduism and Christianity in the sense of falsehood-truth, darkness-light, sin- sanctity, damnation –salvation. He prefers instead of the following pairs; potency-act, seed-fruit, forerunner- real presence, symbol- reality, desire- accomplishment…[222] Thus, he makes collaboration between Hinduism and Christianity.

3.2 Inclusion of Hindu Religious Thought

Panikkar finds no difficulty in integrating Hindu philosophical and religious thought to that of Christian dogma. His hermeneutical stance can be understood as follows; how and how far Indian philosophy can help us to understand and to express Christian dogma.[223] For him Indian philosophical system as an instrument will help in the transformation or rather the conversion of Hinduism itself.

---

[219] R. Panikkar, "Relation of Christians to their Non- Christian Surroundings", *Indian Ecclesiastical Studies (*July-December: 1965): 334.

[220] R. Panikkar, "Indirect Method in the Missionary Apostolate", *Indian Journal of Theology* 19 (July-December: 1970): 111.

[221] K. Dockhorn, "Christ in Hinduism as Seen in Recent Indian Theology", *Religion and Society* XXI/4 (December-1974): 42.

[222] *Ibid.*

[223] R. Panikkar, "The Integration of Indian Philosophical and Religious Thought", *Religion and Society* V/2 (June-1958): 22.

3.2.1 The Idea of Integration

Integration represents more than merely adaptation and adoption. It implies the fact that to speak in the proper language and to think in the language we speak.[224] He affirms that there are two ways of learning a language; the first way proceeds comparing words with words and other way discovers relation between words and things. Integration means to assume really some principles, ideas or attitudes and make not only room for them in a previous scheme, but to convert them- for it is a real conversion- into an integral part of Christian life, tradition and doctrine.[225]

3.2.2 Necessitated Conditions of Integration

Panikkar brings out two conditions of integration: on the one hand understanding of Christian theology and theological understanding of Indian philosophy on the other. For him theology is not a kind of supernatural metaphysics… but a very word of God speaking to men (sic) and the words of men (sic) about God…[226] He, therefore, argues that theology cannot be tied up to any particular class, world or culture. Latter means to say not only that Indian philosophy is a kind of pre-Christian theology (forerunner or substitutes of Christianity) but also that the catholic study and approach must be a theological one.[227]

3.2.3 Principles of Integration

Panikkar understands three kinds of principles: ***firstly,*** Principle of Homogeneity; it is to find out of common ground where integration is possible. For him homology is not analogy and vice versa.[228] ***Secondly,*** Principle of profundity; he uses the word contemplation to substitute with profundity. For him contemplation opens the door of Indian wisdom. ***Finally,*** Principle of tradition; it does not mean that we have to stick at old formulae or that we have to give up all new

---

[224] *Ibid.*, 23.

[225] *Ibid.*

[226] *Ibid.*, 25.

[227] *Ibid.*

[228] *Ibid.*, 27.

thinking and process…but we cannot be limited in our intellectual concern and disregard the history of the past and of the present.[229]

3.2.4 Trinitarian Integration

Trinitarian integration has resonance with threefold classification of Panikkar. And this threefold classification is certainly widespread in the two major sources of Panikkar's thought: the Western and the Hindu tradition. Even in the secular West we find for example, key triadic classification in philosophers from Plato to Comte. In Hinduism we find the *trimurti* of Brahma, Vishnu and Siva, the *trimarga;* Karma, Bhakti and Jnana, the *triguna;* sattva, rajas and tamas, *triloka* and many others.[230] Panikkar is cautious about why he is relating it with trinity. As he remarks, "I am within tradition, although transcending it (as any tradition demands), when I apply this notion to the radical trinity that is to reality, trinity is the measure of all things."[231]

3.3 Legitimization

3.3.1 Common Ground for Christian and Non-Christian Collaboration: A Proposal

Panikkar understands collaboration as the first step for a real partnership. So it is neither concurrence nor competition but co-operation. For him co-operation means common starting point that is an integrally identical ground and a common aim.[232] Because, Christians were not ready to sustain the dialogue and both traditions remained without a common language. It began to seek after a genuinely Hindu- Christian theology. He observes three levels of grounds: this triple foundation corresponds to Christ's threefold function.

---

[229] *Ibid.*, 29.

[230] Varghese Manimala, *Towards Mutual Fecundation and Fulfillment* (Delhi: Media House/ISPCK, 2009), 54.

[231] R. Panikkar, "A Self Critical Dialogue" in Joseph Prabhu (ed.), *The Intercultural Challenges of Raimon Panikkar* (New York: Orbis Books, 1996), 276.

[232] R. Panikkar, "Common Grounds for Christian and Non-Christian Collaboration", *Religion and Society* V/1 (March-1958): 29.

3.3.1.1 Koinonia

According to Panikkar, to be a Christian is neither a privilege nor an excuse to refuse to work in the world...[233] Therefore, the fellowship of Christian with the non Christian world is neither a non Christian nor a neutral relation, nor an artificial make- belief, but an ontic reality based on the *Koinonia* of every being in Christ.[234]

3.3.1.2 Diakonia

For him *Diakonia* is the sacramental level par excellence. Certainly the so-called non-Christian partner may not have the sacramental fullness of the new covenant... but he (sic) shares in the cosmic sacraments of the first pact of God with mankind (sic)...[235] So, Christians must be the ministers of this primeval sacrament.

3.3.1.3 Kerygma

The Christian has received the injection to announce the gospel. For Panikkar the Christian has not primarily to teach morals or even to preach doctrine... but s/he has to proclaim God, His fatherhood, His kingdom, the love which the Christ the Lord taught His disciples to spread.[236] He further argues, for, Christ did not come to found a religion and much less a new religion, but to fulfill all justice and to its fullness every religion of the world.[237] In a word, church brings all true and authentic religion to its fulfillment through a process of death and resurrection, which is the true meaning of the conversion: real Christianity being the fulfillment through conversion of every religion and the mission of the church that of being salt, light, leaven, which gives taste, illumines and raises the whole mass without

---

[233] R. Panikkar, "Relation of Christians to their Non- Christian Surroundings" in (ed.), Joseph Neuner, *Christian Revelation and World Religions* (London: Compare Books, 1967), 163.

[234] *Ibid.,* 164.

[235] *Ibid.,* 166.

[236] *Ibid.,* 167.

[237] *Ibid.,* 168-169.

claiming to be identified with- but neither separated from- the whole cosmos.[238]

Often Christians cannot be faithful to those grounds for they see them to be intrinsically bad and opposed to higher values. Panikkar, therefore, comments that the relation of non-Christian religion with Christianity is not one of the error to truth, darkness to light, evil to goodness, but rather of potence to act, seeds to fruits, type or symbol to the thing and reality in self.[239] If we prefers the former then we extremely level down Christianity to the natural level. On the other hand Panikkar alarms that the seed must die, the symbol must give a way to reality, and the potence must be transformed in to act…[240]

3.3.2 Non-Christian Surroundings: Panikkar's Claims

Panikkar rejects the phrase 'non-Christian' on account of four reasons: (a) it is effective and unacceptable for the so-called non-Christian religions to be described only by a negative feature… the expression is nothing more than …theological colonialism… (b) …it cannot face up to any historical, philosophical or even theological criteria… and (c) ...the expression non-Christian amounts to saying that other religions are false religions…In fact, the so-called non-Christian religions cannot be described for…Christ is already there.[241]

3.3.2.1 Critique of the Christian Attitude

He authentically criticizes the traditional attitudes of Christianity and argues that Christianity has no monopoly of goodness, no monopoly of truth and no monopoly of salvation. Panikkar discards two ways of attitude of Christians: negativism and psychological position. Former, he argues that the Christian is not there to condemn or judge the world but to serve and save it. Panikkar instead prefers

---

[238] *Ibid.*

[239] R. Panikkar, "Common Ground for Christian and No-Christians Collaboration, 35.

[240] *Ibid.* He uses the analogy of rope and snake, surmise it to be snake; snake is merely appearance, it is not real; but it is an appearance of the real, it is reality in the form of an appearance in the status of illusion.

[241] R. Panikkar, "Relation of Christians to their Non-Christian Surroundings" in (ed.), Joseph Neuner, *Christian Revelation and World Religions,* 144-145.

the attitude of true ecumenism or ecumenical ecumenism. In the latter position Christian has simply to witness to Christ without mixed motives. For him the Christian is simply witnessing to a new dimension, hidden or unknown of the same reality. He (sic) has authority neither to condemn nor to escape but to assume and to go deeper.[242]

3.3.2.2 Alternative

Panikkar's alternative is precisely against the so-called *mystique of the incarnation* that is the attitude which advocate the Christian presence everywhere in the world and the *mystique of the transcendence* that is the attitude underlying... supernatural aspect of Christianity.[243] Panikkar slams both attitudes and claims that pure transcendentalism would lead to a kind of mono-dimensional supernaturalism, which is the opposite of Christian revelation; mere incarnationism would become sheer naturalism and fall into an inner worldly activism...[244] This caused Panikkar to use alternative which he calls *mystique of redemption*: in fact there is no redemption without incarnation but neither would redemption have any meaning at all, if it did not lead towards transcendence.[245] This alternative is done in two ways; on the one hand, offering of the sacrifice and receiving the sacrament on the other. Panikkar concludes that the Christian is the priest of the whole of creation and also the priest of mankind (sic) and his (sic) primarily priestly action is that of gathering the materials for the sacrifice...and receives the sacrament from God.[246] Consequently, the so-called non-Christian belongs to the sacramental order and even enters into the Eucharistic economy. If not, a theology is deaf to the environment where it has to live would become very soon also dumb for that milieu.[247] In such kind of endeavor Panikkar is more

---

[242] *Ibid.,* 171.

[243] *Ibid.,* 172-173.

[244] *Ibid.*

[245] *Ibid.*

[246] *Ibid.,* 174.

[247] A. Panikkar, "Indic Theological Series", *Jeevadhara* XVII/ 101 (September-1987): 419.

inclined to Hinduism, preferably Brahmanic form not popular form of Hinduism.

3.4 Influence of Hinduism

3.4.1 Influence of Advaitic Hinduism

3.4.1.1 Advaita

It is not monism but a denial of duality. The Hindu understanding of Advaita is based on what is called *sat-karya-vada* that the reality of the effect pre-exists in, and issues forth from, the cause of its reality. This reality providing cause is called *upadana karana.*[248] According to Sankara, the plentitude of Advaita is the very Brahman is inner mostly present to the creatures as its total cause...[249] It is a category which can be applied to not only for objectifiable experiences, but also for those which are non objectifiable, according to our previous discrimination.[250] The Christian thinkers on the other hand, are convinced that we are so radically infinite that we cannot reach out that intuition without the grace, but they identify the grace with that of Sankara's requirement, elevation. Elevation is an ultimate increase of the Advaita which links us with God.[251] Panikkar would see Advaita as practically symbolizing the Trinity.[252]

3.4.1.2 Panikkar's Re-Interpretation of Advaita Vedanta

Panikkar's basic conception of reality is Advaitic. According to Biren Kumar Nayak though his conception of reality is Advaitic, he moves from Trinitarian spirituality to theandric spirituality and expresses cosmotheandric intuition where he differs from Sankara's Advaita.[253]

---

[248] Cause Providing Realty. (See, Richard De Smet, "Towards a Real Life-Indian Theology- The Advaita of Christianity", VJTR LIX/6 (June-1995): 406.

[249] *Ibid.,* 409.

[250] M. Von Bruck, "Advaita and Trinity", *Indian Theological Studies* XX/1 (March-1983): 43.

[251] *Ibid.*

[252] Dominic Veliath, "The Trinity in Indian Theology", *Kristu Jyoti* 8/2 (June-1992): 17.

[253] B. K. Nayak, "A Critical Study of Christology of Raimundo Panikkar in an Advaitic Frame work' *Bangalore Theological Forum* 38/2 (December-2006), 202.

Panikkar argues that Advaita helps us to understand God and world are not two…and they are one and the same intuition.[254] In Vedanta, the concept of Isvara is one which is put forward to explain the problem of the relation between Brahman and world.[255] Panikkar connects Isvara with that of Christ. He writes; Christians believe that God has become man (sic), but they are afraid to believe that man (sic) is called upon to become God. Hindus are prone to believe the latter, but find the former more difficult-yet Asia is more than these two religions.[256] Yet he builds his theology on the philosophy of Advaita and develops universal synthesis of the three margas of Hinduism. However, problem continues because of his inclination only towards Hinduism still there are other valuable religious traditions co-exist together in India.

3.4.1.3 Influence of Advaitic Spirituality an Panikkar

3.4.1.3.1 Trinity and Advaitic Spirituality

3.4.1.3.1.1 Conception of God

Panikkar understands God only in relation to creatures. For him … God is meaningless without creatures.[257] He goes on to argue "…I would say that God is the Ultimate I, that we are his thous and that our relation is personal, Trinitarian and non-dualistic."[258] Panikkar opines that God and world are neither one nor two…thus no exclusive relationship with God is possible except Advaitic orientation.[259]

---

[254] K. P. Aleaz, *Christian Thought Through Advaita Vedanta* (Delhi: ISPCK, 1996), 162, notes, 907.

[255] K. P. Aleaz, "The Contributions of Advaita Vedanta to Indian Christian Theology in the Second Millennium", *Jeevadhara* XXIX/ 173 (September-1999): 365.

[256] R. Panikkar, "Nine Sutra on the Asian Christ", *Jeevdhara* XXX/177 (May-2000): 334.

[257] D'Sa, "The Notion of God" in Joseph Prabhu, (ed.), *The Intercultural Challenge of Raimon Panikkar,* 42.

[258] *Ibid.,* 43.

[259] R. Panikkar, "Towards an Ecumenical Theandric Spirituality", *Journal of Ecumenical Studies* 5/2 (Summer- 1986): 507.

3.4.1.3.1.2 Conception of Jesus Christ

The climax of Panikkar's Christological formulation, an Advaitic Christology is expressed in his noted work, *The Unknown Christ of Hinduism.* He is convinced that there is a living presence of Christ in Hinduism... Christ is not only the ontological goal of Hinduism but also its true inspirer, and his grace is the leading, through hidden, force pushing it towards its full disclosure.[260] Consequently, Panikkar proposes his Advaitic Christology by introducing the role of Isvara in Advaita Vedanta. He emphatically says in the realm of philosophy; the role of Isvara in Vedanta which postulated in order to explain the connection between God and the world without compromising the absoluteness of the former or the relativity of the latter corresponds functionally to the role of Christ in Christian thought. It is precisely this correspondence that provides Indian philosophy with a locus for Christ and Christian theology for Isvara.[261] Thus, he advocates an Advaitic interpretation of Christ, Isvara, Hence, in Panikkar's perception his cosmic Christology is a philosophical dilemma common to all religious traditions: the problem of relating the transcendent absolute to the finite world.[262] He contends that the function or role of Christ, his personhood as a savior is more important than his spatio-temporal individuality.[263]

3.4.1.3.1.3 Conception of Spirit

He considers Christ as the manifestation of Spirit. He presses further: Christophany takes nothing away from Christology but is open to the reality of the Spirit, which without separating logos from *Pneuma,* does not subordinate the latter to the former.[264] As Christ is the light which acts upon the person in a prehensive union: an advaitin experience. In short, Panikkar understands spirit in relation to Christ

[260] R. Panikkar, *The Unknown Christ of Hinduism,* IX-X.

[261] *Ibid.,* 133.

[262] B. K. Nayak, "A Critical Study of Christology of Raimundo Panikkar in an Advaitic Frame Work", 223, n. 119.

[263] R. Panikkar, *Salvation in Christ: Concreteness and Universality- The Super Name* (California: Santa Barbara, 1972), 72.

[264] R. Panikkar, Christophany: The Fullness of Man, Trans, Alfred D' Lascia (New York: Orbis Books, 2004), 10.

(Pneunmatological Christophany) that is it is openness to the spirit, which manifests Christ and invites meaning- giving reflection (Logos) upon that experience.[265] Above stated Advaitic intuition implies three things, as highlighted by Kuruvilla Pandikattu: all existing beings have their existence depending on Brahman, all existence has meaning in relation to Brahman and all existence, including that all culture, reveals something of Brahman.[266]

3.4.2 Hindu Religious Monograms: Philosophical/Vedantic Influence

In the history of Christian thought theologians tried to express their theology in cryptic symbols which brings out the specific emphasis of their thought.

3.4.2.1 Meaning of Monograms in Theology

John B. Chethimattam upholds following meanings of monograms; ***firstly,*** they represent an easy way for removing certain expressions from common use and reserving them for the sacred.[267] ***Secondly,*** the mysterious character of the object of earth. ***Thirdly,*** the ongoing education of the common people and ***finally,*** these are the strong affirmation of what religion stands for...[268] But a handful of theologians object with this way of giving meaning and others affirm that it is a religious instruction through such a pithy expressions and symbols.[269] In one particular occasion Panikkar ironically observed that one religion cannot be another; and all religions cannot be of equal worth when they teach different things, often contradictory

---

[265] Brad Banon, "Eco-Pneumatology of Raimon Panikkar: Spiritual Life in the Suburbs", *Journal of Dharma* 31/4 (October-December: 2006): 470.

[266] Kuruvilla Pandikattu, "Advaitic Model of Pluralism for India: An Indian Christian Contribution", *JPJRS* 1/1 (January-1998): 139.

[267] For instance, Israel's Kenite storm God- YHWH.

[268] John B. Chethimattam, "Religious Monograms and Mantras", *Journal of Dharma* IX/2 (April-June: 1984): 148-149.

[269] *Ibid.*

things.[270] Later, he changed his view and preferred philosophical ideas of Hinduism for Christian theological interpretation.

3.4.2.2 Brahman

Modern Hinduism understands Brahman not as a person but as the Asolute and thus identified with God. Now two problems arise; on the one hand the relationship of Brahman with Atman and the relationship between Brahman and God on the other. Panikkar, however, deals with the second issue. He goes on to argue that Brahman stands at the end of a philosophical and theological speculation… God on the other hand stands at the end, at the goal of human worship.[271] In this juncture Panikkar connects Atman and Brahman and says that Atman is the soul and Brahman as the world ground.[272] That is how he postulates his idea to that of trinity. In his words, if Brahman is the discovery of the Jnana marga and in a way Atman is the first postulate of the Karma marga, God under whatever name, yet somehow as a personal supreme is the condition and end of the Bhakti marga.[273]

Brahman is the culmination and the goal of the entire Vedic world of its prayers, hymns, and sacrifices. Its superiority is foreshadowed in the Rig Veda and the Atharva Veda. Brahman is far more than a principle satisfying intellectual inquiry; it is the subtle centre of our existence that is consciousness *(Cit)* and also the ultimate joy and bliss *(Ananda)*.[274] The problem arises when we understand different aspects of Brahman. According to Chacko Valiaveettil, Brahman is beyond all speech and thought. No image can represent Brahman and

---

[270] R. Panikkar, "Christ, Abel and Melchizedek", *Jeevadhara* 1/5 (September-October: 1971): 398.

[271] R. Panikkar, "The Brahman of the Upanishads and the God of the Philosophers", *Religion and Society* VII/2 (December-1960): 13.

[272] *Ibid.,* 14.

[273] *Ibid.*

[274] R. Panikkar, *The Vedic Experience; Mantramanjari* (London: Darton, Longman Todd, 1977), 673.

no thought can conceive it. Brahman is *nirguna,* without qualities, *nirvisesa,* without differences and *nirupadhi* unconditioned.[275]

3.4.2.3 Atman

The notion of atman signifies the inner cause, most properly the conscious inner cause and improperly even the unconscious inner cause.[276] For Panikkar atman alone in the Upanishads means the body, the vital divine breath, awareness, the subject of all sensations, and of everything, the independent active subject, the real self in and of man (sic) the self of the world...[277] Panikkar writes that Indeed what is the spirit but the atman of the Upanishads, which is said to be identical with Brahman although this identity can only be existentially recognized... The end of every individual is the recognition that this atman is identical with Brahman.[278] In other words the atman is the connecting link between this *loka* and the Brahma *loka.*[279]

3.4.2.4 Isvara

Panikkar has extensively influenced by the Vedantic notion of Isvara and it is very clear in his understanding of Isvara and Christ. God and the world according to Advaita Vedanta- and the conception is perfectly Christian- are not two... but they are not one either.[280] Brahman as related to the world is Isvara who is *saguna,* with qualities, *savisesa,* with difference and *sopadhi,* conditioned.[281] This

---

[275] Chako Valiaveettil, "The Influence of Advatic Hinduism on Christianity" in Gnana Robinson, (ed.), *Influence of Hinduism on Christianity* (Madurai: TTS Publications, 1980), 17.

[276] R. V. De Smet, "Categories of Indian Philosophy and Communication of the Gospel", *Religion and Society* 10/3 (September-1963): 23.

[277] R. Panikkar, *The Vedic Experience: Mantramanjari,* 698.

[278] R. Panikkar, *The Trinity and Religious Experience of Man-Icon, Person, Mystery* (New York: Orbis Books, 1973), 63-64.

[279] R. Panikkar, "Samdhya the Vedic Prayer", *Indian Theological Studies* XIV/1 (March-1977): 23.

[280] R. Panikkar, "Isvara and Christ as a Philosophical Problem", *Religion and Society* VII/3 (October-1959): 9.

[281] Chacko Valiaveettil, "The Influence of Advaitic Hinduism on Christianity", 17.

tension between Brahman and Isvara is resolved by Panikkar through the introduction of Christ. For this purpose Panikkar quotes *Brahma Sutra 1:1, 2.* The universally accepted meaning is the following: Brahman is that *from which* all things have come forth, *in which* they are maintained and *into which* they will return. In a word… Brahman is the cause of the world.[282] But the problem here arises is whether Brahman and the cause are different or identical? According to Panikkar, cause of the world, Demiurge, Prime Mover, Maker, Divine Power, Isvara or even Creator and the like are not yet Brahman according to vedantism.[283]

Panikkar, therefore, argues that in fact neither dualism nor pure monism can solve this problem.[284] It is true that there is identity and diversity, yet he brings Christian dogma of Trinity to solve this problem and argues that the ontological link between apparently two irreconcilable poles- the Absolute and the Relative is called Isvara, God the Son, the *Logos,* the Christ.[285] Hence, he points out the characteristics of Isvara-*that* or *whence:* ***first of all,*** *yatah* (from which); its proper characteristic is to be a 'from which', an originated in a certain sense, a begotten, an expression, an image.[286] He connects it with *logos*. Even Hindu philosophers acknowledged the dichotomy between Isvara and Brahman. In the words of Sankara, Isvara can still be called God, but he is no more the Asolute, the Ultimate, Brahman, Sankara's Isvara is essentially *saguna*, and yet somehow, pretends also to be *nirguna*. While for Panikkar …he is not only and not primarily a creature, but is equal to Brahman and yet distinct in his form of subsistence.[287] ***Secondly,*** *janamadi* (origin); there is a production, sustenation, etc., of being as such in an intemporal, if not eternal way. In short, Isvara of our *bhasya* fulfills both roles- he is that from which being is, in an intemporal way, and that towards which being becomes, within the temporal process.[288]

---

[282] R. Panikkar, "Isvara and Christ as a Philosophical Problem", 9.

[283] *Ibid.*

[284] Dualism digs a gap and monism oversimplifies it (*Ibid,* 10).

[285] R. Panikkar, "Isvara and Christ as a Philosophical Problem", 12.

[286] *Ibid.,* 13.

[287] *Ibid.*

[288] *Ibid.,* 14.

3.4.2.5 Samdhya

Panikkar derived this term from the Vedas. It literally means holding together, union, junction, juncture and it comes from a prefix *sam,* denoting cumulation, synthesis, reunion and a root *dha* to put, to place; hence *sam* and *dha* together denote to unite, combine, reconcile, mend, put together and similar notions.[289] *Samdhya* sometimes refers to the intermediate state (between this world and the other). For Panikkar, *Samdhya* stands for the meeting of the objective and subjective forms of knowledge, the encounter between human and divine ways of dealing with reality.[290]

3.4.3 Influence of Bhagavat Gita

Bhagavat Gita holds a prominent place among Hindu scriptures. According to P. V. Rane the Gita is also called the fifth Veda.[291] In a word Gita is a song of lord Krishna in the battle field of Kurukshetra. The two margas (Bhakti & Karma) taken by Panikkar are exclusively from Gita which always concerned of integral action. Bhakti marga is elaboratively discussed in Gita. Bhakti marga is the way of ardent devotion, love and abandonment to the lord who is the manifestation of Brahman to man (sic).[292] Gita calls these margas as the way supreme, superior both to the way of sacrifices and to that of the pure ontological knowledge of the Upanishads. For Gita karma is a human necessity and also divine need.[293] Hinduism understands karma in three ways: karma as the saving sacrificial action (Samhitas), karma as the subtle structure of temporal reality (Upanishads) and karma as the path of action of good works (Gita).[294] Panikkar in his explanation of trinity incorporates Gita's understanding of karma. Nishkama karma is an important teaching of the Gita. However,

---

289 R. Panikkar, "Samdhya the Vedic Prayer", 24.

290 *Ibid.,* 26.

291 James Canjanam Gamaliel, *Dharma in the Hindu Scripture and in the Bible* (Delhi: ISPCK, 1997), 25. Cited from, P. V. Rane, *History of Dharma Sastra,* Vol: 1 (Pune: Bhandakar Oriental Research Institute, 1930), 126.

292 R. Pankkar, *The Vedic Experience: Mantramanjari,* 424.

293 *Ibid.,* 425.

294 *Ibid.,* 540.

Panikkar understood that karma marga, the way of sacred action that is ritual action leading to salvation, the fulfillment of duty, realization of one's dharma, obedience to the law keeping of the commandments...[295] Since, mutual fecundation is the central theme of Panikkar, he wants to make nexus between trinity and karma. In the words of Panikkar a Christian can believe in karma and a Hindu in trinity.[296]

3.4.4 Upanishadic Influence

The Upanishadic teachings are predominantly influenced on his doctrine of trinity. The Upanishad contains the *mahavakya* which is considered the zenith of Upanishadic teaching. The saying of *chandogya Upannishad* is notable here: *ekam evadvitiyam* (One without a Second). It transcends and negates the duality. That is why he borrows the idea of Jnana and connects it with Christian understanding of the Spirit. For Panikkar, knowledge here is obviously not a merely epistemic or abstract cognizance of a certain state of affairs, but the total Jnana, the perfect and conscious realization of what Brahman is: the Real, the Truth, the One.[297] He goes on to affirm that it posits the primary of the One in an incontrovertible manner, so that Advaita stands for a full and uncompromising oneness.[298] This is vividly underscored in the third person of the trinity.

3.5 Hindu-Christian Theology: Panikkar's Query

It is obvious that there are two phases of Indian theology; ***first of all,*** reformulating the pre-existing Christian theology in Hindu terminology and ***secondly,*** creating an Indian Christian theology. Panikkar says three words (Hindu, Christian and Theology) are somewhat unsatisfactory: for, theology does not correspond to any Hindu concept, the word Hindu is imperfect (bundle of religion) and the word Christian is also improper, for Christianity possesses a

[295] R. Panikkar, *The Trinity and Religious Experience of Man-Icon, Person, Mystery,* 16-17.

[296] R. Panikkar and Abraham Koothottil, "Man and Religion: A Dialogue with Panikkar", *Jeevadhara* XI/ 61 (January-February: 1981): 32.

[297] R. Panikkar, *The Vedic Experience: Mantramanjari,* 653.

[298] *Ibid.,* 657.

jungle of theologies...[299] So, he prefers the word *Rtatattva.* According to him *Rtatattva* could be the word expressing the awareness, the goodness and establishment (embracing Jnana, Bhakti, and Karma) of the right order of things.[300] Hence, he articulates a genuine Hindu-Christian theology wherein we see a radical propensity towards Hinduism. But it is justified in such a way that it is especially to Hindu intellectuals. According to T. K. Thomas to understand Christ and His message...transmit it into non-Christian friends in a language and idioms familiar to them... .[301] At present no one can claim that Brahmins only are the intellectuals and he overlooked a vast majority of mass in India, called subalterns.

Conclusion

Above discussed analysis tells the fact that Panikkar is influenced by Advaitic, Upanishadic, and Philosophical Hinduism and even by Bhagavat Gita. It is obvious that many Christians when told that the Christian teaching about God is non-dualistic (Advaitic) are incredulous, chiefly for two reasons: because in their prayer they are used to address God as the Superior being and they are rather Christo-centric at least in their imagination. Introducing God in Advaitic color is vehemently opposed by even Indian Christian theologians mainly for two reasons: one is that they cannot accept the view that Christian theistic concept of God is inferior to the monistic concept of God; the other is that Brahman is devoid of qualities.[302] A. J. Appasamy goes little further and argues that we must reject any kind of Advaita which depersonalizes God.[303]

Panikkar's whole understanding is centered on his mystical apprehension of reality. Walter Capps therefore, states: his (Panikkar's)

---

[299] R. Panikkar, "Rtatattva: A Preface to a Hindu Christian Theology", *Jeevadhara* IX/49 (January-February: 1979): 9.

[300] *Ibid.*

[301] T. K. Thomas, "Gospel, and Indian Intellectuals Today", *Religion and Society* XIV/4 (September-1967): 44.

[302] H. Vanlalauva, "God in the Contemporary Christian Thought", *Mizoram Theological Journal* 2/2 (July-December: 2000): 10. Cited from, M. M. Thomas, *The Theology of Nehemiah Goreh (*Madras: CLS, 1969), 54.

[303] *Ibid.* Cited from, R. Boyd, *Indian Christian Theology,* 129.

scholarship is largely a product of the transposition of mystical aspirations into methodological- yes methodological objectives...[304] Hence, Panikkar's theological vision poses serious problem and hints at intriguing possibilities. In the words of Dominic Veliath, since religion is personalized as a symbol, and situated in the realm of orthopraxis rather than orthodoxy...[305] However, many of the focal categories which underpin Panikkar's vision have either a non-dualistic connotation or non-dualist nuances. But the category of non-dualism seems to defy these categorizations and straddles these divisions, since it involves inclusivism and pluralism, Christo-centrism and Theo-centrism. So it definitely calls for clarification and articulation. Because, Panikkar himself has rightly pointed out that theologizing in India is not an exegesis of past texts but the expressing from the recess of the Indic people of the ineffable experience of the living faith.[306]

His wrong use of integration may lead to syncretism which continues the problem as long as Christ is in the scene thus either we Christianize or we Hinduize it. While this is the case the doctrine of trinity is irrelevant for the subalterns who are more or less free from so-called Brahmanic traditions. In short, Panikkar is advocating a lukewarm interpretation of any tradition and a dilution of the incisiveness of any religion.

---

[304] Dominic Veliath, "God and Religions- Indian Approaches", *Kristu Jyoti* 15/1 (March-1999): 46. Cited from, W. Capps, "Towards a Christian Theology of the World Religions", *Crosscurrents* (Summer- 1979): 168.

[305] *Ibid.,* 53.

[306] R. Panikkar, "Indian Christian Theology", *Jeevadhara* XXVII/161 (September-1997): 319.

Chapter 4

A Subaltern Critique on Hindu Hegemonic Theology of Panikkar

4.0 Introduction

India needs a living theology not a hinduized theology. A living theology is not that addresses itself to the questions, aspirations and sufferings of a people in a given situation. Panikkar's theology excludes these realities and perpetuates Hindu hegemonic theology. To critique Panikkar's theology in this context marked by serious conflicts and contradictions demands a clear option. It is an option for life, and a pledge to withstand forces destructive of life in all its forms-the nature and the human beings particularly the poor and the weak. This chapter makes critique on his understanding of Hinduism and Indian Christian theology especially Panikkar's theological frame work, methodology and theological articulation.

4.1 Subaltern Critique

4.1.1 The Term Subaltern

The word subaltern, first of all, has both political and intellectual connotation. Its implied opposite is of course dominant or elite…[307]

[307] Edward W. Said, "Forward" in Ran jit Guha and Gayatri Chakravarthy (eds.), *Selected Subaltern Studies* (New Delhi: Oxford University Press, 1988), v.

Subaltern has become a fashionable word among the academics today. Subaltern constitutes the mass of the laboring population as distinguished from the elite in India.[308] Though, the original meaning refers to an officer of an inferior rank…it points to social groups. Subordination is one of the two constitutive terms in a binary relationship of which the other is dominance.[309] The most widely accepted meaning that the subaltern- the socio-economically (religiously also) inferior, marginalized, oppressed and downtrodden people- is a comprehensive term that includes people whose inferiority is differently based: on gender, on birth, on family lineage, on social status, on the economic strength, etc.[310]

Subalternity is a polyvalent term that can be understood in many ways. Its origin can be traced back to Antonio Gramsci (1891-1937), the Italian thinker, who used the word subaltern in two senses: In one sense by subaltern he meant the code word for the industrial proletariat…In the second sense in a general way the relation of domination and subordination in class divided societies.[311] The Dalits constitute, perhaps the most important and comprehensive category of the subalterns.

4.1.2 Subaltern Critique

It is true that subalterns are deliberately marginalized by the caste Hindus and imposed on them Hindu world view that continuously seek to demean, disrupt and destroy their communal life. Sathianathan Clarke argues that this may call for a conscious process of de-sanskritization…There was an historical period in which Indian Christians attempted to project a false Brahmanical

[308] Ranajit Guha and Gayatri Chakravarthy (eds.), *Selected Subaltern Studies,* (New Delhi: Oxford University, 1988), vi.

[309] Rudolf Heredia, "Subaltern Interrogation of Hindu Nationalism II", *VJTR* 66/11 (November-2002): 916.

[310] Johnson Puthenpurackal, "Philosophizing from the Dalit Perspective" in George Thadathil (ed.), *Subaltern Perspectives: Philosophizing in Context* (Bangalore: ATC Publications, 2005), 24.

[311] Prakash Louis, "The Meaning of Subaltern : A Socio-Philosophical Discourse" in George Thadathil (ed.), *Subaltern Perspectives: Philosophizing in Context,* 48.

identity by copiously drawing upon classical Hindu symbols, rites and philosophical themes in recent years we have to reclaim our subaltern and non Brahmin heritage.[312] It invites subaltern religio-cultural aspects into Christian theology which will involve bringing back joy, jubilation and celebration even if in the midst of suffering and oppression.[313] Because from the heads of creative minds (elites) theology is produced and orthodoxy is defined. Any religious situation that demands or effects this collusion becomes a problematic site of interreligious and inert community celebration.[314] In short, subaltern critique attempts to recognize the voice of the subalterns starts with the deconstruction of the theological imperialism and elitism by letting the reality of the subalterns speak.[315]

4.1.2.1 Subaltern Critique: Integration or Autonomy

There was at the down of the century two diverging paths open to the subaltern people. On the one hand integration into a reformed Hinduism with Sanskritization; and a rejection of the Brahmanic tradition with an assertion of autonomy.[316] Here, one may ask how can a subaltern (Dalit) person critique dominant theologies? Anthoniraj Thumma proposes following tips: a) analytical dimension-theologians' key to analysis is the caste Hinduism and b) critical dimension-many theologians describe subaltern theologies as critical reflection on people's life experience of suffering, struggles and liberative praxis.[317] Subaltern hermeneutics underline all these facts.

---

[312] Sathianathan Clarke, "Dalit Christian Worship: A Theological Reflection", *Masihi Sevak* XXII/4 (December-1997): 17.

[313] *Ibid.*, 18.

[314] *Ibid.*, 22-23.

[315] Felix Wilfred, *Margins: Site of Asian Theologies* (New Delhi: ISPCK, 2008), 103.

[316] Rudolf Heredia, "Subaltern Interrogation of Hindu Nationalism I", *VJTR* 66/10 (October-2002): 831.

[317] Anthoniraj Thumma, *Wisdom of the Weak: Foundation of People's Theology* (Delhi: ISPCK, 2000), 172.

4.1.3 Subaltern Hermeneutics

Generally hermeneutics is what is meant is the intellectual discipline that probe into the very nature and presuppositions of understanding human expressions M. A. Devasia understood subaltern hermeneutics is three ways: ***First;*** to analyze, to clarify and thereby attempting at the resolution of the conceptual issues that surround explanation and interpretation without losing sight of their context-sensitivity, ***second;*** to establish logical connection between meaning, truth and validity and ***third;*** to discover the philosophical significance of a subaltern reading of the logic of practice that constitutes linguistic activity in general and religious language in particular.[318]

4.1.3.1 Subaltern Hermeneutics as Post Colonial Deconstruction

The post colonial era poses threats to human life in the Asia: caste-class discrimination, rich-poor polarity, internal and external conflicts, marginalization of vast segments of people, women's subordination, corruption at the high places and other related evils.[319] Sahayadhas by citing Sugirthrajah, argues that Christian theology in Asia has responded to these issues in two ways: compliment and conflict. Postcolonial hermeneutics likes to be associated with the second which based on the revolt against dominant. Its main agenda is oppositional, critical, prophetic and paradoxical activity with the enslaved.[320] It takes side with the poor, marginalized, exploited, oppressed, etc.[321] Postcolonial theologians in Asia move beyond the territories of biblical scholarship into the realm of symbols, images

---

[318] M. A Devasia, "Subalternity and Hermeneutics of Religious Language" in George Thadathil (ed.), *Subaltern Perspective: Philosophizing in Context*, 106.

[319] R. Sahayadhas, "Christian Theological Hermeneutics in Asia: Prospects and Problems in Constructing Contextual Theologies", *Bangalore Theological Forum* XXXV/1 (June-2003): 157-158.

[320] *Ibid.*

[321] Subaltern hermeneutics fosters following principles: a) Interpreter (participation in the struggle), b) Location (experience), c) Earthliness (which indicates an inseparable interconnection between their religious world view and their actual world of experience, and d) The orality of sources over against written sources as mark of accuracy… (*ibid*, 161).

and myths/stories.[322] So, Sathianathan Clarke projects drum as the symbol to have a comprehensive view of subaltern theology. S. Clarke goes on to argue that this sort of theology must move beyond the sterility, passive fatalism, anti-humanism and anti-normativism...[323]

For Rudolf Heredia subaltern hermeneutics will not suppress any of these voices or refused to give them a hearing but will rather listen to them all against the horizon of our own conceptual presuppositions and value commitment, and still be open to the possibilities of a fusion beyond these.[324] In short, subaltern hermeneutics at the beginning tries to question the dominant hermeneutics and then seek a fusion of horizons beyond the clash of perspectives of both. Fundamental aspect of this is that the text must be read from the perspective of the poor; the praxis and actual involvement of the interpreter is a decisive factor in the interpretation.[325]

4.1.4 Subaltern Critique on Religion and Hinduism

A subaltern thinks religion was responsible for all the evils in the society. They, therefore, claim that religion should rationally be evaluated from the perspective of human life. S. Robertson of the opinion that any religion or religious practices that obstruct human dignity should be abandoned.[326] Periyar summarizes religion as follows; a) Religion as a way of life in this world...b) there is no supernatural element in religion, c) the spiritual dimension of religion is the work of human mind and d) there is no divine element in humanity.[327] It is true that all the inequalities and oppressions found in the society were created by priestly religion.

---

[322] R. Sahayadhas, "Christian Theological Hermeneutics in Asia: Prospects and Problems in Constructing Contextual Theologies", 161.

[323] S. Clarke, "Constructive Christian Theology: A Contextual Indian Proposal", *Bangalore Theological Forum* XXIV/1, 2 (March-June: 1997): 105.

[324] Rudolf Heredia, "Subaltern Interrogations of Hindu Nationalism I", 831.

[325] Juan Alfara, "God Protects and Liberates the Poor- OT", *Concilium* (October-1986): 29.

[326] S. Robertson, "Periyar E. V. Ramaswamy's Critique of Priestly Hinduism and Its Implications for Social Reforms", *Religion and Society* 49/2, 3 (June-September: 2004): 11.

[327] *Ibid.*, 18-19.

Periyar realized that Hinduism places of all kinds of hooliganism where human person was not valued, instead caste was given priority. He presses further that the worst untruth that is in circulation is the claim that there is a religion called Hinduism.[328] As M. M. Thomas remarks, for him (Periyar) Hinduism is founded by Brahmins for their own power interests; they built on ignorance, illiteracy and poverty of the people and exploited them.[329]

In this chapter the expression priestly Hinduism is used as a synonym for Brahmanic Hinduism. Dharma Theertha defines Brahmanical Hinduism as a system of socio-religious domination and exploitation of the Hindus based on the caste, priest craft and false philosophy-caste representing the scheme of domination, priest craft the means of exploitation and false philosophy a justification of both caste and priest craft.[330] Unfortunately, Indian Christian theologians aided the interpretations of Brahman by taking concepts only from Vedas and Upanishads. At this juncture subaltern critique vehemently slams their authenticity, validity and veracity. On the other hand Brindavan C. Moses comments that Brahmanical religion has contributed to the democratization of Indian society by enforcing religious authority and religious sanctions and practices…[331]

4.2 Panikkar's Hindu Hegemonic Theology

Panikkar is convinced of the presence of Christ in Hinduism. So he proposes Christian interpretation of Hindu scriptures and holds that a solution to the theological and philosophical inquiries of Indian

---

[328] *Ibid.* Cited from, E. V. R. Periyar, *Man and Religion* Trans. By R. Sunder Raju (Madras: Rationals Publications, 1993), 17.

[329] *Ibid.* Cited from, M. M. Thomas, *The Secular Ideologies* (Madras: CLS, 1976), 128.

[330] S. Robertson, "Periyar E. V. Ramaswamy's Critique of Priestly Hinduism and Its Implications for Social Reforms", 20. Cited from Swamy Dharma Theertha, *History of Hinduism Imperialism* 5th Edition (Kerala: Ambedkar Foundations, 1992), 6-7.

[331] Brindavan C. Moses, "Brahmanism, A Hindrance to the Emergence of a Vibrant Civil Society and the Establishment of Human Right and Dignity for Dalits, Tribals and Women in India", *Religion and Society* 47/3 (September-2000): 43.

tradition would be found in the trinity.[332] A. M. A. Ayrookuzhiel condemns the Indian Christian Theological reflections for accepting the dominant Hindu versions without questioning their identity and purpose ignoring their context and the folk versions and traditions.[333]

4.2.1 Hinduized Theology

The precise question one may ask is why Panikkar and other Indian Christian theologians did not use subaltern religion at least once in their theological enterprise. Robert Deliege gives following guessed reasons: a) subaltern (Dalit) religion lacks reflectively and depth and thus it is rooted in ignorance…and b) it is related more with local demons and non-hierarchical relationship within themselves…[334] Since 1980s theological arena has been undergoing many changes and in the national realm as well. According to K. C. Abraham the emergence of organized movements of Dalits, Tribals and other marginalized sectors, and their determination to do theology drawing on their experience of oppression and hardship as well as their spirituality is a new watershed in Indian theology.[335] It has posed a serious challenge to traditional hinduised theology.

But the path of Vedantic thinking can seriously undermine the participation of the subaltern in the making of theology. Anderson Jeremiah summarizes following reasons; ***firstly,*** the Vedas that stem from the deep structure of *Varnashrama Dharma*, the undemocratic and unjust social system prescribed by Manusmriti and ordained by divine religious practices has no place for them…If we follow the path,

---

[332] Joseph P. Pinto, *Introduction through Basic Communities: An Indian Perspective* (Bangalore: ATC, 1985), 99.

[333] A. M. A. Ayrookuzhiel, "Dalit Theology: A Movement of Counter Culture" in James Massey (ed.), *Indigenous People: Dalits* (Delhi: ISPCK, 1994), 261.

[334] Sathianathan Clarke, 'Dalit Religion as a Resourceful Symbolic Domain: A Critical Review of Theories of Religion and a Constructive Proposition to Glean the Riches of Dalit Subjectivity", *Religion and Society* 49/2, 3 (June-September; 2004): 35. Cited from Robert Deliege, *The World of Untouchables: Paraiyars of Tamilnadu* (New Delhi: Oxford University Press, 1998), 252.

[335] K. C. Abraham, "Re-Interpretation of Christian Tradition in Contemporary India", *AJT* 9/2 (October-1995): 267.

God becomes obsolete for the oppressed.[336] ***Secondly,*** if the Vedic paradigm is given full authority in understanding and interpreting Jesus to the Indian religious context, it raises a serious question; from a subaltern point of view, it means coloring the perpetuation of inhuman life and exploitation under the Vedic prescription of caste system with a Christian message.[337] ***Finally,*** Panikkar's Pluralistic methodology, which assumes all religions have the same essence, is problematic. A. Jeremiah opines that all religions have their own way of understanding the essence of their own religion.[338]

4.2.2 Allegations

Subalterns have made two major allegations on Indian Christian theology: a) it appears to be exclusionary and non-dialogical by turning a deaf ear to the collective religious resources of the Dalits and, b) it fosters the hegemonic objections...[339] The main drawback with Indian Christian theology was that it predominantly used the religion of literacy to retell the Christian story of Jesus and to remember the Indian heritage that testified to the Christic presence among them.[340] Subalterns have been under a suffocating experience, for the Dalits, by being made the objects have not only been given little or no attention in history, but have been subjected to extreme form of dehumanization.[341] In this sense Panikkar's theology is dehumanized theology.

---

[336] Anderson Jeremiah, "Introduction: A Subaltern Critique of K.P Aleaz's Indian Christian Vedanda", *AJT* 21/2 (October-2007): 406.

[337] *Ibid.,* 407.

[338] For instance, existence of body at the final state of liberation- Christianity recognizes the resurrection of body and bodily existence after resurrection. He also explains the concept of *Karma and Samsara* Christianity doesn't share it. He concurs that this process (endless cycle of birth and death) has been the cause of suffering for millions of shudras (subaltern people), blaming it upon their *Karma* in their previous births (*Ibid.* 407).

[339] K. P. Aleaz, "Some Features of a Dalit Theology", *AJT* 18/1 (April-2004): 151.

[340] *Ibid., 155.*

[341] Johnson Puthenpurackal, "Philosophizing from the Dalit Perspective" in George Thadathil (ed.), *Subaltern Perspective: Philosophizing in Context,* 38.

4.2.3 Can Panikkar's Theology be Astika?

Looking at a standard text book on Indian Christian theology, one can say that the roots of the current Indian theological expression are in the experiences of mostly upper caste converts. James Massey rightly observes that these high caste converts' immediate concern was how they should relate or interpret their new faith or experience in Indian thought forms, that is based on the Brahmanic religion and culture in which they had grown.[342] Like other Indian Christian theologians, Panikkar too interpreted Christian faith based on Astika school of thought (Vedas, Upanishads, and Shad Darsana, etc.). And it did not address the issues[343] of the majority Christians. In the words of Wesley Ariarajah: "one of the disturbing features of theology until now has been that they have had little or no impact on the theology of the pulpit and the pew."[344] Arvind Sharma, therefore, asks can Christian theology be regarded as authoritative from the point of view of any of the orthodox schools of Hindu philosophy.[345]

4.2.3.1 Panikkar's Theology – Theology from 'Above'

Panikkar uses enormous philosophical categories in his writings. As we are in the post modern era philosophy must be criticized, for having been cut off from the realities of real and practical world. According to Johnson Puthenpurackal philosophy is now no more considered as an intellectual luxury of an elite group of intellectuals, for philosophy has been brought down after the death of Hegel.[346] Indian Christian philosophizing has to give priority for the questions of the subalterns (adjectival Dalits)…and their dreaming expressed in

---

[342] James Massey, "Need of a Dalit Theology", *CTC Bulletin* XVII/2 (April -2001): 72.

[343] Life situation of oppression, poverty, suffering, injustice, illiteracy and denial of identity (*Ibid.* 73).

[344] Wesley Ariarajah, "Asian Christian Theological Task in the Midst of other Religious Traditions", *CTC Bulletin* XVIII/1 (April-2002): 15.

[345] A. Sharma, "Can Christian Theology be Astika?", *Indian Journal of Theology* 37/2 (1994): 11.

[346] The death of Hegel as the end of modernity and the beginning of post modernity, Johnson Puthenpurackal, "Philosophizaing from the Dalit Perspective", 42.

the form of folk stories and folk dances, poems and ballads paintings and sculptures, proverbs and riddles, street plays and dramas…[347]

4.2.4 Why Did Panikkar not Use Subaltern Religion for Theologizing?

Panikkar in his whole endeavor tries to understand Brahmanic religion as a resources for doing theology and completely sidelined majority religion in India. Felix Wilfred talks about three elements in subaltern religion: a) the world of spirits, b) the emergence of gods and goddesses from the contexts of life and c) the super imposition of the religiosity of the dominant castes and classes.[348] Damayanthi Niles in her article cites Berlinerblau the sociologist, who gives three possible reasons of why theologians exclude popular religion (subaltern) in their theological task? ***Firstly,*** scholars of the subject have come from diverse academic disciplines. ***Secondly,*** the study of popular religion has come around the same time as the post modern movement, which rejects the use of meta systems to describe a subject. ***Finally,*** the sheer diversity of types...[349]

4.3 Critique on Panikkar's Hindu Hegemonic Theology

Here, arises a fundamental question is it possible for a theologian who belongs to one particular religious faith to feel at home and participate on another? Exploring this question at an abstract level the answer would probably be no. M. Amaladoss on the view that when people encounter another tradition…the normal tendency is to try to integrate them into one's own tradition through a process of reinterpretation and adaptation.[350]

---

[347] Johnson Puthenpurackel, "Philosophizing from the Dalit Perspective", 42-46.

[348] Flex Wilfred, "Subaltern Religious Experience", *Journal of Dharma* XXIII/1 (Jan-March: 1998): 59-62.

[349] Damayanthi Niles, "The Study of Popular Religions and our Theological Task", *AJT* 18/1 (April-2004): 214.

[350] M. Amaladoss, "Double Religious Belonging and Liminality", *VJTR* 66/1 (January-2002): 22.

4.3.1 Panikkar's Methodology

Down through the centuries theologians have been used numerous theologizing methods.[351] Panikkar used the method of Interculturation not exactly Inculturation the way in which he proposed the same was known as homeomorphic methodology based on pluralistic perspective. Ogden refers pluralism as a transformation of human existence, from self centeredness.[352] For Panikkar given the fact that symbols, signs, etc. are part of a cultural or religious system or text, the cross cultural and cross religious hermeneutics would engage itself in finding out homeomorphic symbols or concepts, namely, symbol or concept playing an adequate role and function in another religions or cultural system.[353] Thus, Christian theology was cast in the Indian molds of Vedanta, Jnana marga, Bhakti marga and Karma marga. According to A. Thumma the original meaning of the biblical message and Christian experience was better understood by the appropriation of and reinterpretation in the Indian religio-cultural symbols, thought pattern, theological categories and style of life.[354] Whereas problem with Panikkar is, he is confined to Brahmanic traditions; in spite of other religions. But this method harbors many shortcomings; a) It strives to indigenize the apologetical method without challenging the western method which Panikkar characterizes as Christianity's religious superiority and church's immunity and supra culturality.[355] b) This is oriented to the past and threats Christian theology and the Indian culture as static realities.[356] c) It is selective; it narrows down Indian culture to Brahmanic sanskritic culture of the elite

---

[351] For instance, apologetical method (Missionaries), cultic model (Orthodox), Scriptural model (Reformers), dogmatic (R. C), experiential – praxis method (Modern Theologians) and dialogical and inculturation method (Contemporary Theologians, Particularly Panikkar). Anthoniraj Thumma, *Wisdom of the Weak: Foundation of People's Theology,* 74.

[352] M. Ogden, *Doing Theology Today (*Pennsylvania: Trinity Press, 1996), 177.

[353] R. Panikkar, *The Intra-Religious Dialogue* (New York: Paulist Press, 1978), 55.

[354] *Ibid.,* 78.

[355] R. Panikkar, "Indic Christian Theology of Religious Pluralism from the Perspective of Inculturation" in K. Pathil (ed.), *Religious Pluralism: An Indian Christian Perspective* (Delhi: ISPCK, 1991): 271-272.

[356] F. J. Balasundaram, *EATWOT in Asia* (Bangalore: ATC, 1993), 16-17.

high class cast…hence this method was perceived to be promoting hinduization and brahmanization, and the cast inequality and gender discrimination of the oppressive Brahmanic hegemony.[357] d) Culture is treated bereft of its context- perceived solely in conceptual, static term of abstract philosophy and religious rituals.[358] Thus, this form of theology has become irrelevant to the changing vibrant Indian context, especially to the struggling marginalized groups. Dialogical method or Interculturation (of Panikkar) too mostly has tended to be elitistic and selective in its dialogue neglecting the subaltern groups and blind to the pain of the oppressed and their traditions…[359] Lancy Lobo reiterates that Indian culture is pluriform pertaining to different religions and various ethnic groups such as Dalits, Tribals and other subalterns peoples of little traditions and folk cultures.[360]

4.3.1.1 Subaltern Methodology

Subaltern theology has introduced experiential- praxis method as their corner stone thereby it is purely hermeneutical, analytical, dialectical, critical and creative (in its reality). But the outbreak of liberation theology has posed a unique methodology which instead of beginning from the text, here theologizing springs from the context…here theologizing is not based on the philosophical theory or a theological maxim; it is based on liberative praxis.[361] For this subaltern group act more as agents and servants of the theologizing process. In the words of M. Amaladoss …Asians tend to start with their experience and with the complexity…this starting point makes their reflection not abstract, but context-sensitive. If the experiential basis is not noted this might easily seem relativistic…[362] In this sense subaltern theologies are liberative and critical.

---

[357] *Ibid.,* 80.

[358] Felix Wilfred, *Sun Set in the East-Asia Challenges and Christian Involvement* (Madras: University of Madras, 1991), 177-178.

[359] Anthoniraj Thumma, *Wisdom of the Weak: Foundation of People's Theology,* 84.

[360] Lancy Lobo, "Towards an Introduction in the Non-Sanskrit Tradition, *VJTR* 49/1 (January-1985): 16.

[361] Anthoniraj Thumma, *Wisdom o the Weak: Foundation of People's Theology,* 94.

[362] M. Amaladoss, "Proclaiming the Gospel", *VJTR* 57/1 (January-1993): 29.

K. C. Abraham proposes following features of this theology; a) it raises critical awareness of the people vis-à-vis their situation of bondage, b) they reject the dominant theology…, c) they produce vision for the future and empower people to change the existing values and relationships and, d) they are integral to people's ongoing search for their identity and their struggle for justice.[363] It is the juncture where Panikkar deserves criticism. Paul Knitter concedes that it needs to be grounded and inspired by a preferential option for the suffering and victims of this world. He further elaborates but if our criterion for judging what is true or false, good or bad, is no longer, is it in the Bible or the Upanishads or the Koran but rather does it remove human suffering and promote life…[364] This is very evident in the theological articulation of Nirmal when he criticizes: "broadly speaking, Indian Christian theology in the past has tried to work out its theological systems in terms of either Advaita Vedanta or Vishishta Advaita… the result has been that Indian Christian theology, has perpetuated within itself what I prefer to call the Brahmanic tradition…one wonders whether this kind of Indian Christian Theology will ever have a mass appeal.[365] Subaltern methodology goes in line with EATWOT which states that we reject as irrelevant and academic type of theology that is divorced from action…[366]

4.3.2 Panikkar's Theological Framework

Attempts have been made from the last century to develop an Indian Christian theology starting from Hindu religious thought. For Felix Wilfred that entire one does here is to replace the Western

---

[363] K. C. Abraham, "Re-Interpretation of Christian Tradition in Contemporary India", 268.

[364] Paul Knitter, "Cosmic Confidence or Preferential Option?", *Bangalore Theological Forum* XXIII/4 (December-1991): 23.

[365] A. P. Nirmal, "Towards a Christian Theology" in James Massey (ed.), *Indigenous People: Dalits,* 215.

[366] K. C. Abraham (ed.), *Third World Theologies: Commonalities and Divergences* (Bangalore: EATWOT, 1995), 206.

philosophical language with an Indian one.[367] He presses further: "we do not have to make a plastic surgery on theology to give it an Indian look."[368] The basic concern of this line of thought is to create a Hindu Christian theology, a reflection of faith which Hindus and Christians can share together.[369] Theologizing in India, Panikkar understands that theology as a human activity is intrinsically depending on its historical situation.[370] Unfortunately, his theologizing process is heavily depending on Hindu spirituality rather than historical situation.

4.3.2.1 Hindu Spirituality Vs Subaltern Spirituality

Panikkar used Brahmanic spirituality as a framework to interpret trinity to Indian minds. India is traditionally known to be a land of spirituality. It does not mean that everything in India is spiritually sound or that India need not a critical evaluation of its own spirituality. It does not have significant to the subalterns and it is precise to quote Gnana Patrick as he rightly concurs:

In the Indian context, the so-called mainstream Hindu spirituality, if it is convinced in a linear progression as the movement which leads from the Vedas and Upanishads through the Bhagavat Gita to the great Bhakti movement will remain distant from the subaltern spirituality. Even the marga centered practical spiritualities of the Indian religions do not seem to resonate with the spirituality of the subalterns. The Sadhana of the Jnana which in a step by step spiritual journey, is to lead the human beings to the realization of the Brahman, the Upasana of the Bhakti marga which by meditating on the name of the personal god, Isvara proceeds to the Sayuja (intimacy with the Lord), and the Nishkama Karma of the Karma marga,

---

[367] Felix Wilfred, "The Problem of a Valid Starting Point for Theologizing in India" in M. Amaladoss, T. K. John and G. Gispert Sauch (eds.), *Theologizing in India* (Bangalore: TPI, 1981), 138.

[368] *Ibid.,* 141.

[369] John B. Chethimattam, "Problems of an Indian Theology: A Critique of Indian Theologizing" in M. Amalados, T. K. John and G. Gispert Sauch (eds.), *Theologizing in India,* 201.

[370] R. Panikkar, "Indian Theology: A Theological Mutation" in M. Amaladoss, T. K. John and G. Gispert Sauch (eds.), *Theologizing in India,* 30.

which, emphasizes the way of action do not seem to correspond to the spiritual traditions of the subaltern people...[371]

And subaltern spirituality is born in the 'thick of struggles' over against Upanishadic and monastic spirituality of the Indian tradition. Brahmanic spirituality is oriented towards interiority by the spirituality of the subaltern is oriented towards exteriority, the lived out mundane world of life and it is attempting to experience the power of God in the world of action and struggles.[372] For feminists (women) Subaltern spirituality is often being characterized by three different terminologies: subversion of dominant discourses, transgression of the legitimacy and the transcendence of human limitation.[373]

4.3.3 Theological Verbalization

What struck in Panikkar's theology is the Hindu character of the theologizing. Panikkar's collaboration between Christ and Isvara proves the fact that the Christian faith will permeate India only as a part of Hinduism this is what Herbert Hoefer calls "Christ-ized Hinduism."[374]

4.3.3.1 Christology: The Point of Departure

As John G. Arapura notes Panikkar makes a daring attempt to show that, although the concept of Isvara devised by Vedanta to explain the reality of the world under the category of transcendent Brahman is the basis, it leaves several problems unsolved...[375] Panikkar uses later philosophy (Isvara) most viable to speak of the Father and the Son and he asks a question: where do Hinduism and Christianity

---

[371] Gnana Patrick, "Subaltern Religions and Spirituality" in George Thedathil (ed.), *Subaltern Perspectives: Philosophizing in Context,* 138-139.

[372] *Ibid.,* 140.

[373] Gabriel Dietrich, *A New Thing on Earth* (New Delhi: ISPCK, 2004), 238-249.

[374] Herbert Hoefer, "Jesus My Master: Jesu Bhakta Hindu Christian Theology", *Dharma Deepika* 8/1 (Jan-June: 2004): 5.

[375] John G. Arapura, "Re-Thinking Christianity in India: An Assessment of Indian Attempts", *Jeevadhara* XXIII/136 (July-1993): 287.

meet?[376] His fundamental principle is that we must refrain from judging and rejecting one religious tradition merely because it does not conform to our already crystallized and obstinately established doctrines. Contrastingly, John Cobb argues that God provides and guides our ways to newness of life by means of most diverse traditions of mankind (sic) not only Hinduism.[377] Sahayadhas makes two considerations on Panikkar's Christology: this perfectly conforms to the Advaitic frame work but not to the Christian understanding of God and …the concept of God in these traditions stand as polar-opposites (dualism vs. non-dualism).[378]

In fact, in this theological elucidation, the historicity of Jesus has seemingly no place as it does not have a place for the phenomenal reality. In the Vedantic thought identical with *Brahman* is given more importance. Jesus did not consider it as a privilege of being one with the Supreme Being or Pure Consciousness, but emptied himself and took the form of a servant, *jiva* and sacrificed himself for humanity. Panikkar affirms that the role of Isvara of the Vedanta corresponds functionally to the role of Christ in the Christian thought, thus Hinduism has a place for Christ and Christian theology has space for *Isvara.* Here, Christian theology cannot start with the historicity of Christ. For Panikkar, the scriptural narratives about Christ begin not with flesh but with *logos.* Sahayadhas is of the opinion that our Christological starting point cannot be the *logos* but the flesh because it is the flesh that represents the fleshly that is the suffering humanity.[379]

---

[376] R. Panikkar, "The Unknown Christ of Hinduism" in John Hick and Brian Hebblethwaite (eds.), *Christianity and Other Religions* (Britain: William Collins Sons, 1980), 122.

[377] John B. Cobb, "Mystical Pluralism" in Joseph Prabhu (ed.), *The Inter-Cultural Challenge of Raimon Panikkar* (New York: Orbis Books, 1996), 46.

[378] R. Sahayadhas, "Perspectives in Christological Reconstructions: An Explorations of the Writings of Select Theologians", *Bangalore Theological Forum* XXXVIII/2 (December-2006): 130-131.

[379] *Ibid.,* 130.

4.3.3.2 Brahman – God

As Panikkar is influenced by *Brahma Sutra Bhasya* of Sankara, he interprets Brahman to be upper caste god. The importance question that comes up here is: Does Panikkar's conception of the Brahman make sense of the linguistic space of the subalterns? The paradigmatic notion here is that of *adhyasa*[380] or superimposition. It means the act of cognizing something as some other thing.[381] It is clear from the above quote, the cognition of the embodied self and in that the subaltern self can operate only when *adhyasa,* the mutual superimposition of the self and the non-self is presupposed. It radically clarifies when one considers the Advaita conceptualization of realty at two levels: they are the *Paramarthika Sattuva* (Absolute Reality as in the case of non-dual Brahman) and the *Vyavaharika Sattuva* (Relative Reality as in the case of objects) in our waking experience such as myself, others, trees, tables, etc.[382]

There seems to be a big difference between the Christian understanding of God and Advaitic Brahman. Christian God is a personal God and not a static of being or consciousness. For biblical God acts historically in the world but for Brahman phenomenal world is an illusion. Panikkar's God, however, leaves us with a God who is unknown, unknowable (*Nirguna Brahman-* the impersonal God who is beyond human experience). It raises both epistemological and methodological questions. Is not Panikkar guilty of being blatantly selective and reductionistic in his methodology? In addition to this, Subhash Anand observes that while apophatism is a necessary dimension of all theology, it cannot become the only approach to the divine at least not in Christian theology. Hence, the Christian theologians need not offer any apology in using a

---

380 It is the preface of the Brahma Sutra, which is the hermeneutic key to understand the self.

381 For Sankara one superimposes the characteristics of the body when one has such ideas as I am fat, I am thin, I am fair, I say, I go or I scale. So also one superimposes the attributes of the internal organ *(Manas)* possessed of the idea of ego, on the self, the witness of everything, (M.A Devasia, "Subalternity and Hermeneutic of Religious Language", 108. Cited from, Sankara, *Brahma Sutra Bhasya,* Trans. by Swamy Gambhirananda, 4th Edition (Calcutta: Advaita Ashramam, 1983), 6.).

382 M. A. Devasia, "Subalternity and Hermeneutic of Religious Language", 108.

concrete and history – bound language to reflect on his/her faith...[383] Brahmanazing Christian God, therefore, is problematic to many. G. A. Oddie asks does Brahman immerse in the so-called Sanskritic or classical tradition share anything in common with the great mass of the population...[384]

4.3.3.2.1 Brahman - Atman - God - Christ: A Bone of Contention

In Advaita Vedanta *Brahman* is clearly mentioned as the Ultimate Consciousness, while *atman* is a manifestation of it which is partly represented by *jiva.* Ramprasad observes that ...*Brahman* cannot be an object of knowledge, so the very concept of growing in the knowledge of God is impossibility in Advaitic thought. To understand further, he notes that *Brahman* is one: it is not a 'He', a personal Being, nor is it an 'it' an impersonal concept.[385] It proves that *atman* is part of Absolute Reality and has no relevance outside of it.

4.3.3.3 Advaita Vedanta

M. A. Devasia has made decisive criticism on the use of Advaita Vedanta. He observes as follows:

"The dichotamic view regarding 'self delineates the fact is that the dialectical tension between two different and in a sense conflicting ways of conceptualizing the embodied self in the Advaitic paradigm. This implies what I call Advaitic reductionism and furtherer indicates a kind of hermeneutic violence by which the subaltern is disrobed of his/her identity...and more significantly this goes against the very foundational truth of the Advaita itself that all is self (Brahman). Counter to this understanding I argue that a possible genuine

---

[383] S. Anand, "Mahisa- Mardana: A Myth of Holistic Liberation Theology" in Paul Puthanangady (ed.), *Towards Indian Theology of Liberation* (Bangalore: Indian Theological Association, 1986), 71.

[384] G. A. Oddie, "The Dynamics of Popular Religion within Hinduism- The Case of Hook-Swinging Rituals" in David. C. Scott and Israel Selvanayagam (eds.), *Re-visioning India's Religious Traditions* (Delhi: ISPCK, 1996), 86.

[385] A. Jeremiah, "Inculturation: A Subaltern Critique of K. P. Aleaz's Indian Christian Vedanta", 404. Cited from, C. Ramprasad, *Knowledge and Liberation in Classical Indian Thought* (New York: Palgrave, 2001), 173.

Advaitic reading of the subaltern would be such that it constitutes a transformative encountering of the subaltern experience of self embodiment."[386]

Panikkar holds another view in this respect: "a living church in India is the fruit of the re-enactment of the transtemporal mystery of the incarnation: a fecundation between the spirit and the Indian matrix."[387] It reveals the fact that Panikkar's Indian matrix means only Brahmanical Hinduism or Advaita Vedanta. On the other hand J. R. Timm states that the syncretistic tendency of Advaita Vedanta, because it undermined the authority of incarnation and revelation, never received endorsement from the theistic school.[388] So we need not accept uncritically the hegemonious presuppositions and pattern of thought which have guided our predecessors. Thus, *theology of fulfillment* soon became the *theology of mutual fulfillment* which gradually leads to integration of Advaitic experience into Christianity. An integration of Bhakti, Jnana and Karma margas with a certain preponderance of Jnana marga reaching its culmination in a theandric reality...[389]

4.3.3.4 Atman

Panikkar is influenced by Sankara's concept *Aham Brahmasmi* for his theological interpretation. M. A. Devasia purports the crux of the matter as follows: "how are we to connect the notion on the non-dual self with that of the body? If we hasten to say that the self is not body at all, then this linguistic expression would subvert the very ontological and logical truth of the Advaitic paradigm that the self is."[390] It is clear in the dialogue that took place between a *Chandala*

---

[386] M. A. Devasia, "Subalternity and Hermeneutic of Religious Language", 113.

[387] R. Panikkar, "The Dream of Indian Ecclesiology" in G. Vanleeuwen (ed.), *Searching for Indian Ecclesiology* (Bangalore: ATC, 1984), 37.

[388] Jeffry R. Timm, "Vallabha, Vaishnavism and the Western Hegemony of Indian Thought", *Journal of Dharma* XIVI/1 (January-March: 1989): 20.

[389] Antony Mookenthottam, "Ground Work for Indian Christian Theology", *Journal of Dharma* XIV/4 (October-December: 1989): 345.

[390] M. A. Devasia, "Subalternity and Hermeneutic of Religious Language", 110.

and Sankara.[391] This dialogue itself, therefore, nullifies the aspect of using this thought in Indian Christian theology.

4.3.4 Critique on Dharma

Dharma both as a religious doctrine and a spiritual vision for practical living, remains a core element of the classical Sanskritic religio-philosophical world of India. The concept of dharma was a weapon in the hands of the dominant to legitimate and maintain the ascriptive caste order.[392] But several socio-religious movements began to emerge subverting, re-enterpreting and challenging the understanding of the classical dharma. Michael Maher opines that the old dharma, rooted in Hindu religious thought provided ideological support for the caste system and the untouchable's inferior position within that system.[393] Felix Wilfred rightly observed that Brahmanical religious sophistry and swotleties through which humiliation and injustices were heaped on those of low birth...[394]

4.4 Does Panikkar's Theology Really Gasp for Breath?

The theology of Panikkar in fact gasping for breath still it is getting suffocated and constricted by the narrowness of the theological ambit in which it is moving. Indian Christian theology has emerged through the cross fertilization between Christianity and Hinduism

---

[391] In Kasi on an occasion while Sankara, accompanied by his disciples, was going towards the Ganga for a holy bath and prayers, he saw a *Chandala* with ferocious dogs coming across his path and shouted to him: move away! Move away! But the *Chandala* replied: ...when you shouted move away, were you addressing the body or the self? How does such differences as this is a Brahmin; this is *Chandala* arise in non-dual experience? Sankara immediately recognized the truth of this and replied...I am at once abandoning the notion 'this is an out caste'... (*Ibid.* 112. Cite from, K. S. Murty, "What We Owe to Sankara" in R. Balasubramaniam and Sibajiban Bhattacharya (eds.), *Perspective of Sankara* (New Delhi: Department of Culture- Govt. of India, 19890, 444.

[392] Gnana Patrick, "Subaltern Religions and Spirituality", 155.

[393] J. Michel Maher, "Agents of Dharma in a Worth Indian Village" in J. M. Maher, (ed.), *The Untouchables in Contemporary India* (New Delhi: Rawat Publication, 1998), 17.

[394] Felix Wilfred, *From the Dusty Soil: Contextual Reinterpretation of Christianity* (Madras: University of Madras, 1995), 117.

and came to be known as indigenous theology at first, meaning a theology developed in the context.[395] As Panikkar states: "the crisis of religion cannot be overcome from one single religion, and certainly not from one single culture, the task is today urgently cross-cultural that is interreligious, because of the inextricable link between culture and religion.[396]

As Panikkar is concentrating on cross-fertilization between Christianity and Hinduism, he overlooked Asian realities. For Felix Wilfred the horizons of dialogue need to be widened, starting from a change in the very location from where we approach the interrelationship of religion. Religions have to meet at the arena of Asian realities.[397] Therefore, starting point for any theologizing must be experience of the people, which may have following characteristics: it is collective, it is pluralistic, it is unwritten and it reconciles dichotomies.[398]

4.4.1 Indian Christian Theology at the Intersection

In recent decades there have been some remarkably serious effect to give Christianity in India a genuine Indian expression in its spiritual and theological aspects. The classical attempts of the pioneers were mostly to indianize/brahmanise Christian theology in terms and categories of the Vedas and Vedanta. Such attempts in their spiritual quest generally subscribed to one of the three classical Indian ways, viz. Jnana, Bhakti and Karma. Doing Christian theology, therefore, in the context of other religious traditions is not a new enterprise in India. Dayanchand Carr criticizes that in the recent past when indigenization was the great fad of Christians who had suddenly

---

395 C. H. Srinivasa Rao, "The Three Margas of Salvation In Indian Christian Theology' in Anand Amaladoss, (ed.), *Christian Contribution to Indian Philosophy* (Madras: CLS, 1995), 160.

396 R. Panikkar, "A New Society for a New Millennium", *Journal of Dharma* XXVII/1 (Jan-March: 2002): 5.

397 Felix Wilfred, *Sun Set in the East-Asian Challenges and Christian Involvement,* 228.

398 Traditional theology has often caused number of dichotomies- Reason and Faith, Tradition and Scripture, Pastoral and Academic, speculative and Practical, etc., Felix Wilfred, "The Problem of a Valid Starting Point for Theologizing in India", 144-145.

become conscious that they are Indian and not British or American began to uphold the example of De Nobili with mad enthusiasm. A clear example as how not to contextualize theology! Because, the privilege of theologizing had passed from the hands of the Western masters to the Indian upper cast elite.[399]

Classical Christian theology is incapable of grasping the Indian sense or reality. But they rooted in the multifaceted religiosity of our people. According to Amalorpavadoss to the Indian, religion and philosophy are inseparably interfused. Philosophy is a religious vision; and religion is a philosophy lived. Hence, the use of philosophy minus (other) religions can only impart a mere cerebral thrust to the theology of religions.[400] This really causes Indian Christian theology at the cross roads and it necessitates subaltern theology which according to Antony Kolencherry, is a theology in India which must have the imprint of Indian culture, language and society.[401] The criticism was often voiced, usually from within church circles that the church was surreptitiously becoming an established church, seeking linkages with the powers-that-be and catering to elite group in society, while neglecting the weaker sections.[402] Robin Boyd's *Introduction to Indian Christian Theology* has become something of a classic, does not refer to a single subaltern theologian. Clearly there was a serious imbalance that may well be described as a form of hegemonic dominance, to use S. Clark's words. Thus, the neglecting of subaltern forms of Indian Christian faith, and the imbalance in favor of expressions of faith from higher castes converts is now being vigorously rectified in theological circles in India.

---

[399] Dayanchand Carr, "A Biblical Basis for Dalit Theology" in James Massey (ed.), *Indigenous People: Dalits,* 233.

[400] S. Arulswamy, "Liberation Theology in India", *Indian Theological Studies* 22/3 (September-1985): 281. Cited from, D. S. Amalorpavadoss (ed.), *The Indian Church in the Struggle for a New Society* (Bangalore: NBCLC, 1981), 44.

[401] Antony Kolencherry, "South Indian Contribution to Sub Alternative Theologies", *Indian Theological Studies* XL/2 (June-2003): 128.

[402] Lionel Fernandes, "Changing Perceptions of Indian Christians", *JPJRS* 2/2 (July-1999): 158.

4.4.2 From Latin Captivity to Brahmanic Captivity

Like other Indian Christian theologians, Panikkar is based his theological articulation on classical Hinduism that is margas with which he sidelined the folklore, which is the classical text of subalterns. For Felix Wilfred the traditional theology too would belong to the classical realm-which is distancing from experience through the process of abstraction, whereas folklore leads us to the heart of the experience of the people.[403]

Classical theologizing poses following serious problems: a) the doctrines are formulated in the philosophical categories of a particular culture (Hindu), b) it elevates one culture as the norm for the whole church. Joseph Mattam keenly observes as follows: "in the name of Inculturation we may impose one of the specific cultures of a country ...for example, in most of the efforts in India...the Sanskrit tradition and symbols were taken and presented as the one Indian culture. The cultures of the Tribals, Dalits and of the marginalized in general were left out."[404] Thus Brahmanical thought forms have pre-occupied the theologians.

Roger E. Hedlund, therefore, contends, "Indian Christian theology has been shaped by Vedanta rather than by the popular folk religion of the masses."[405] Similarly, S. K. Chatterjee changes that even as a Sanskritization process has served to absorb and suppress the minorities...to an extent where Dalits, Tribals and others have been danger of losing their identity instead of losing their chains.[406] F. Wilfred notes that one of the primary tasks of Asian theology is to

---

[403] Felix Wilfred, "The Challenge of Folklore to Indian Theologizing", *Jeevadhara* XXIV/139 (January-1994): 62.

[404] Joseph Mattam, "Witnessing to Christ through a Relevant Theological Language: An Indian Approach to a New Language in Theology", *Jeevadhara* XXXV/207 (May-2005): 194.

[405] Roger E. Hedlund, "Subaltern Movements and Indian Churches of Indigenous Origins", *Journal of Dharma* XXIII/1 (Jan-March: 1998): 9.

[406] Saral K. Chatterjee, "Indigenous Christianity and Counter Culture", *Religion and Society* XXXVI/4 (December-1989): 10.

draw from the popular religious resources, and re-interpret them for the liberative praxis in the Asian societies.[407]

In the words of Israel Selvanayagam, the Latin captivity referred to at the beginning seems to have been replaced by a Sanskrit captivity.[408] It is subalterns who helped to come out of this captivity. As Clarke mentions ...God was debugged of all the conceptual and metaphysical riddles of reason and scattered into the body of politics of specific marginalized communities.[409] In short, once Indian Christian theology was under Latin captivity but now potentially it is being captive to the Brahmanic traditions of India. Theologians have therefore been characterized it by different names viz. 'dangerous Brahmanic hegemony'[410] and Sanskrit captivity. R. Boyd concludes that we must beware of any captivity which would separate us from our primary captivity to Christ.[411]

4.5 Towards Life – Centric Theology

According to Ivy Singh, the nature of the existing theological orientation in India has been criticized by Indian Christian thinkers as it cannot provide an effective basis for social action and reflection and it often tend to be fixed, logical and systematic but not always empirically or socially true.[412] Thus, Indian Christian theologians found a dynamic role for theology in relation to the socio, economic, cultural, political and religious life experience of the subalterns-women, Dalits, Tribals, etc. to make theology to be relevant in

---

407 Felix Wilfred, *Sun Set in the East- Asia Challenges and Christian Involvement,* 204.

408 Israel Selvanayagam, "Waters of Life and Indian Cups: Protestant Attempts at Theologizing in India" in Sebastian C. H. Kim (ed.), *Christian Theology in Asia* (New York: Cambridge University Press, 2008), 65.

409 S. Clarke. "Subalterns, Identity Politics and Christian Theology in India" in Sebastian C. H. Kim (ed.), *Christian Theology in Asia,* 274.

410 Eric J. Lott, "Hindu Theology's Forgotten Struggles" in Israel Selvanayagam (ed.), *Moving Forms of Theology: Faith Talk's Changing Contexts* (Delhi: ISPCK, 2002), 76.

411 R. Boyd, "Beyond Captivity" in Israel Selvanayagam (ed.), *Moving Forms of Theology: Faith Talk's Changing Contexts,* 124.

412 Ivy, *Voices from Narmada: Doing Eco-feminist Theology* (New Delhi: ISPCK, 2009), 194.

Indian context. If the theology in India desires to expediate the total liberation of human beings from every discrimination and oppression, the theologians should give up traditional boundaries and should take praxis as an important prerequisite for life centric theology.

Having felt this need many Indian Christian thinkers came forward in theological articulation based on subaltern experiences. Traditional theology was by and large a product of western theology which is exclusively carried away by the realities of subaltern life. Their broken spirituality challenges old notions of spirituality, for it begins with the reality of impasse- suffering, pain, poverty, oppression, marginalization, etc.[413] For Lancy Lobo caste has become a divisive and oppressive reality; it fragments society, isolates group from group and places one on top of the other.[414]

It is true that it has hardly addressed the needs of subaltern people especially the weaker section of society-women, Dalits and Tribals. For Ivy Singh, people's painful experiences and their songs and stories are most of the times not taken care of by the theologians.[415] Panikkar's theology is largely rooted in the religious experience of the upper castes. Thus it failed to capture the aspirations of subalterns. Therefore, at present India needs life centered theology. According to M. Stephen theology (Christology) based on Advaita is not relevant. It should include the struggle, pain, desires and hopes of the majority of the people.[416]

Since, spirituality is the integral wholeness of person, it concretizes his/her faith through their daily life experience. So, C. H. Kyung contents that Asian women spirituality is grown out of their daily struggles for full humanity…[417] When feminists' theologians

---

[413] C. H. Kyung, *Struggle to be the Sun Again: Introducing Asian Women's Theology* (New York: Orbis Books, 1990), 86-87. Cited from, Stella Faria, "Feminist Spirituality: Emerging Trends' *Consultation on Asian Women Theology* (1987), 3-4.

[414] Lancy Lobo, "Caste Dynamics", *Jeevadhara* XI/63 (May-June: 1981): 193.

[415] Ivy, *Voices from Narmada: Doing Ecofeminist Theology*, 198.

[416] M. Stephen, 'A Dalit Christology", *Faith Theological Review* VI/2 (September-2003): 25.

[417] C. H. Kyung, *Struggle to the Sun Again: Introducing Asian Women's Theology*, 85-86.

begin to give emphasis on women's spirituality, Dalit theologians concentrate on pathos or sufferings of Dalits. A. P. Nirmal rightly concurs that pain or pathos is the beginning of knowledge.[418] In the words of Georg M. Nalunakkal Dalit theology in India stands over against the dominance of the Brahminic tradition in the so called Indian Christian theology.[419] Since, traditional theology is unnoticed the subaltern consciousness, tribal theology centered on subaltern consciousness. According to Nirmal Minz, the sub-altern consciousness should represent the consciousness of an oppressed nationality in our country. This consciousness is of anger, rejection and protest of the existing dominant socio-economic, political and religious situations in India.[420] The fundamental thrust of life-centric theology is that it solely built on the reality of impasse, pain and pathos and finally on subaltern consciousness. Thus, it accompanies with the poor and marginalized especially in their struggles, sufferings, etc. and it calls for a 'departure' in traditional theology particularly from deductive method to inductive method. Ivy Singh discerns that inductive methods starts from experience and develop ideas and principle from our experience of life in the world.[421] In India theology must be understood in relation to life. For life centered paradigm, according to Ivy is, inclusive because it brings all God's creation as all groaning for liberation.[422]

Conclusion

It seems that Panikkar's pluralistic paradigm and dialogical methodology leads one to domestication or trivialization or privatization or sectarianization of Christian faith. For this fact has been forgotten by Panikkar while translating Christian trinity in Hindu

---

[418] A. P. Nirmal, "Doing Theology from a Dalit Perspective" in A. P. Nirmal (ed.), *A Reader in Dalit Theology* (Madras: Gurukul Publications, 1989), 141.

[419] George Mathew Nalunakkal, *New Beings and New Communities: Theological Reflections in a Post Modern Context* (Thiruvalla: KCC/EDTP, 1998), 10.

[420] Nirmal Minz, "Dalit- Tribal: A Search for Common Ideology" in A. P. Nirmal (ed.), *Towards a Common Dalit Theology* (Madras: Gurukul Publications, 1992), 105.

[421] Ivy, *Voices from Narmada: Doing Eco-feminist Theology*, 206.

[422] *Ibid.*, 294.

terms and categories. So, Panikkar can definitely be called *Sankara* of Christian theology. From subaltern perspective Christianity seems to be the one of the religions offering some hope to the marginalized communities. But Panikkar destroys that hope and paves way for further perpetuation of exploitation and legitimization of subjugation. Leaving the inherited ancestral paradigm and its models aside, a few daring Indian theologians seriously sought for new paths that respond adequately to the Indian situation and needs and are embedded in the local culture. It is important that the religious world of the Dalit and marginalized is re-collected and re-remembered.[423] This fact is gravely highlighted by Walter Fernandes as he concurs: "a genuine people related theology begins with an option in favor of those who are otherwise excluded by the powerful..."[424] This unanimously proves the fact that Panikkar's theology is really gasping for breath in India since *life centered paradigm* has totally been unnoticed by him in his theological articulation.

[423] K. P. Aleaz, "Some Features of a Dalit Theology", 152. Cited from, S. Clarke, *Dalits and Christian Subaltern Religion and Liberation Theology in India* (New Delhi: Oxford University Press, 1999), 2.

[424] Walter Fernandes, "Inter Religious Dialogue from the Perspective of Poor", *VJTR* 59/2 (February-1995): 103.

General Conclusion

The present research work is undertaken with the aim of finding out whether or not the Indian thought (Hinduism) has influenced the Christian thought of Panikkar. It is true that Panikkar's theological contemplation emerged out of three contexts: socio-political, religio-cultural and philosophical contexts. So, his theological enterprise emerged in the perspective of Interculturation. For him, Intercuturation is not to set a world view of one tradition but... lets the two perspectives interact and awaits the outcome of the encounter to take shape and find expression...[425] Therefore, Panikkar can be Characterized as 'world theologian' of our time. He remains as a philosophical theologian who is in search of finding and affirming the meeting point between Christianity and Hinduism. B. K. Nayak writes: "his search for the meeting point engages him in a consistent exercise to show the interrelatedness between the intercultural challenges and to build a bridge on plurality of religions especially in Christianity and Hinduism"[426] or mutual fecundation of religions which he elaborates in the doctrine of trinity.

Panikkar avoids traditional terminology but finds his clue in the three traditional types of spirituality or margas of Hinduism. The correlation of three margas with that of trinity is understood as 'Advaitic Intuition' of Panikkar. It is significant to note that Panikkar

[425] Biren K. Nayak, "A Critical Study of Christology of Panikkar in an Advaitic Framework", *Bangalore Theological Forum* 38/2 (December-2006): 197. Cited from, Anand Amaladoss, "Interculturality as the Source of Raimon Panikkar", *Satyanilayam Chennai Journal of Interculturality Philosophy* 5 (February-2004): 37.

[426] *Ibid*, 211.

advocates a new council, not a Vatican III but a second Jerusalem. A. M. Mundadan observes as follows: "it was through the first Jerusalem council the door was opened for the Jewish Christianity to the Greek world which in course of time became the predominant influence for Christianity to take a particular shape. Through the second Jerusalem Council the predominantly Western form of Christianity must open itself to the Asian world with its culture, philosophies, religions etc."[427]

It is true that Panikkar opened the way to Asian cultures, philosophies and religions but not at least once to Asian realities. Antony M. concedes that often Western thought is expressed in Indian terms rather than Indian thoughts in Indian categories.[428] Others criticize him for his approach of interpreting paganism by means of Christian concepts that is for misinterpreting it, instead of criticizing it for Christian apologetic.[429] Hence, Panikkar's theological approach in philosophical orientation invites critical appraisal by scholars. For, he makes universal synthesis of three margas of Hinduism, not any popular religious traditions.

Panikkar illustrates his view point using the metaphor of colors and rivers and the oceans. All colors are derived from the ray of white light and different rivers symbolize different religions flowing into the same ocean.[430] For which he uses an ambiguous language and sometimes states his views in a cryptic way-jarringly new terms, neologisms, hyphenation of words (Re-velation, Dia-logue, etc.) and the nuances which he brings in the use of words, concepts, ideas and symbols are liable to misunderstanding and thus lead to provoke criticism. It is nothing other than sheer 'verbal terrorism'. Here, what Gispert- Sauch says is a saving factor: "words used by Panikkar are questioned in terms of what they directly meant in the Western theological tradition. In this, one may be closed to the rich world of

---

[427] A. M. Mundadan, *Paths of Indian Theology* (Bangalore: Dharmaram Publications, 1998), 113.

[428] Antony Mookenthottam, "Ground Work for an Indian Christian Theology", 347.

[429] A. M. Mundadan, *Paths of Indian Theology,* 113.

[430] R. Panikkar, "The Integration of Indian Philosophical and Religious Thought", *Religion and Society* 5 (June-1958): 16-27.

dvani, suggestion, allusion, which is precisely the forte of Panikkar's theological semantics. One may hear what Panikkar says but miss what Panikkar whispers.[431]

Karokaran qualifies his critique by asserting, Panikkar represents a paradigm change in the Christian approach to other religious traditions. He can be only judged and appreciated within this changed perspective...[432] According to Andreas Nehring "one problem I see is that the terms pluralism and pluralistic are not only used in their descriptive sense that describes a certain pluralistic reality in which we find ourselves, but they are also used as an ideology, as a way of relating to this reality."[433] In this entire endeavor Panikkar is highly influenced by priestly Hinduism and therefore, his theology is hinduized which deserves liberation from Brahmanic captivity. In the words of Eric Lott 'the liberation is possible when we are casting off false identities, false conditioning, and finding our true identity.'[434] Panikkar's theology, therefore, has to consider following stipulations:

Decanonization: The canonizing tendency of official religion reveals itself also in its understanding of God...consequently as a very distant God.[435] F. Wilfred notes that ...the fundamental religion that is sectarian, closed and dogmatic.[436] K. P. Aleaz views that it is not simply enough for Indian Christian theology to champion the inclusion of the subaltern communities; it must also create space

---

[431] G. Gispert Sauch, Review of Christ the Mystery in History: A Critical Study of the Christology of Panikkar, by Cherian Menacherry, *VJTR* 60/12 (December-1996): 899.

[432] Anto Karokaran, "Raimond Panikkar's Theology of Religions: A Critique", *VJIR* LXIII/10 (October-1994): 669.

[433] Andreas Nehring, "The Prodigal Son's Religious Grounding: Questioning Pluralistic Theologies" in David. C. Scott and Israel Selvanayagam (eds.), *Re-visioning India's Religious Traditions,* 175-176.

[434] Eric Lott, *Religious Faith, Human Identity: Dangerous Dynamics in Global and Indian Life* (Bangalore: ATC/UTC, 2005), 293.

[435] Subash Anand. "The Liberative Potential of Popular Religious Traditions" in David C. Scott and Israel Selvanayagam (eds.) *Re-visioning India's Religious Traditions,* 100.

[436] Felix Wilfred, *Sun Set in the East-Asian Challenges and Christian Involvement,* 197.

for their particular mode of expressing and communicating their reflection.[437] It is true subalterns' rich communal religious reflectivity is expressed in non-textual or non-scriptive forms that is music, painting, dance, weaving, songs, architecture, etc. Clarke points out that Theo-logia, in India has to become inclusive of Theo-graphic and Theo-phonia.[438]

Despiritualization: The official religion emphasizes the moral and functional values of faith while de-emphasizing its mystic, symbolic and festive dimensions. Thus, spoke men (sic) of elite religion tend to be guilty of un-dimensional interpretation of life and religion.[439] Because, subaltern values of faith are overlooked and this must be restored through the organizing symbol of drum as it reflects a subaltern based culture or philosophy which rooted on orality.

Decentralization: The major religions of the world are basically power institutions. Hindu religion is centralized in the areas of ethical code, theology and rituals.

Demythologization: The myth of pure ancestry too is unmasked. Jesus was totally negating the claim of Pharisees that they are the true descendents of Abraham (cf John: 8).

Accordingly, Panikkar has to re-interpret and re-write and deconstruct-reconstruct his theological articulations and interpretations in order to get perennial weight from the subaltern people at large. If not, he is making a theology of caste Hinduism, for Sanskrit was limited to the twice born castes and subalterns not permitted to learn Sanskrit and thereby gospel is devalued, experience of the vast majority is disdained and Christian faith is hinduized and Christian theology is brahmanized. Thus, the author has to finally conclude that Panikkar's theology is influenced by Hinduism to a considerable extent.

---

[437] K. P. Aleaz, "Some Features of a Dalit Theology", 152.

[438] *Ibid.* (writings and voices) cited from, S. Clarke, *Dalits and Christian Subaltern Religion and Liberation Theology in India,* 21-22.

[439] Subash Anand. "The Liberative Potential of Popular Religious Traditions", 102.

Bibliography

I. Primary Sources (Works by Panikkar)

Books

Panikkar, R. *The Unknown Christ of Hinduism* London: Darton, Longman, Todd, 1964.

________. *Religion y Religions* Madrid: Editorial Gredos, 1965.

________. *The Trinity and World Religions: Icon, Person, Mystery* Madras: CLS, 1970.

________. *Salvation in Christ: Concreteness and Universality- The Super Name* California: Santa Barbara, 1972.

________. *Trinity and Religious Experience of Man* New York: Orbis Books, 1973.

________. *Worship and Secular Man* London: Orbis Books, 1973.

________. *The Vedic Experience: Mantramanjari* London: Darton, Longman, Todd, 1977.

________. *The Unknown Christ of Hinduism: Towards an Ecumenical Christopany,* Revised Edition. Bangalore: ATC, 1982.

________. *Myth, Faith and Hermeneutics: Cross Cultural Studies* Bangalore: ATC, 1983.

________. *Intra-Religious Dialogue* Bangalore: ATC, 1984.

________. *The Cosmotheandric Experience: Emerging Religious Consciousness* Delhi: Motilal Banarsidass, 1998.

________. *The Fullness of Man: A Christophany,* Translated by Dilascia Alfred. Delhi: ISPCK, 2006.

Articles

Panikkar, R. "Relation of Christians to their Non-Christian Surroundings" in Joseph Neuner (ed.), *Christian Revelation and World Religion* London: Compare Books, 1967.

________. "The Meaning of Christ's Name in the Universal Economy of Salvation" in Joseph Pathrapankal (ed.), *Service and Salvation* Bangalore: TPI, 1973.

________. "The Unknown Christ in Hinduism" in John Hick and Brian Hebblethwaite (eds.), *Christianity and Other Religions* Britain: William Collins Sons, 1980.

________. "Indian Theology: A Theological Mutation" in M. Amaladoss, T. K. John and G. Gispert Sauch (eds.), *Theologizing in India* Bangalore: TPI, 1981.

________. "The Dream of Indian Ecclesiology" in G. Vanleeuwen (ed.), *Searching for an Indian Ecclesiology* Bangalore: ATC, 1984.

________. "The Dialogical Dialogue" in F. Whaling (ed.), *The World's Religious Traditions* Edinburgh: SCM, 1984.

________. "The Jordan, The Tiber and The Ganges: Three Kairological Moments of Christic Self Consciousness" in John Hick and Paul F. Knitter (eds.), *The Myth of Christian Uniqueness: Towards a Pluralistic Theology of Religions* New York: Orbis Books, 1988.

________. "Indic Christian Theology of Religious Pluralism from The Perspective of Interculturation" in Kuncheria Pathil (ed.), *Religious Pluralism: An Indian Christian Perspective* Delhi: ISPCK, 1991.

________. "A Self Critical Dialogue" in Joseph Prabhu (ed.), *The Intercultural Challenge of Raimon Panikkar* New York: Orbis Books, 1996.

________. "Introduction" in Varghese Manimala (ed.), *Towards Mutual Fecundation and Fulfilment of Religions* Delhi: Media House/ ISPCK, 2009.

Journals

Panikkar, R. "The Integration of Indian Philosophical and Religious Thought" *Religion and Society* V/2 (June- 1958): 22-29.

________. "Common Grounds of Christian and Non-Christian Collaboration" *Religion and Society* V/ 1 (March-1958): 29-36.

________. "Isvara and Christ as a Philosophical Problem" *Religion and Society* VII/ 3 (October-1959): 8-16.

________. "The Brahman of the Upanishads and the God of the Philosopher" *Religion and Society* VII/2 (December-1960): 13-16.

________."Hinduism and Christianity" *Religion and Society* VIII/ 4 (December- 1961): 10-18.

________. "Relation of Christians to their Non-Christian Surroundings" *Indian Ecclesiastical Studies* (July-December: 1965): 330-337.

________. "Church and World Religions" *Religion and Society* 14/ 2 (June-1967): 59-63.

________. "The Internal Dialogue- The Insufficiency of the so called Phenomenological Epoch in the Religious Encounter" *Religion and Society* 15/3 (September-1968): 55-66.

________. "Metatheology or Diacritical Theology as Fundamental Theology" *Concilium* 6/5 (June-1969): 21-27.

________. "Indirect Methods in the Missionary Apostolate" *Indian Journal of Theology* 19 (July-December: 1970): 111-113.

________. "Faith- Constitutive Dimension of Man" *Journal of Ecumenical Studies* 8 (Spring-1971): 221-232.

________. "Faith and Belief: A Multifarious Experience" *Anglican Theological Review* 53 (1971): 314-329.

________. "Christ, Abel and Melchizedek" *Jeevadhara* 1/ 5 (September-October: 1971): 391-403.

________. "God of Silence" *Indian Journal of Theology* 21 (1972): 121-128.

________. "The Category of Growth in Comparative Religion: A Critical Self Examination" *HTR* 66/1 (January-1973): 113-140.

________. "Have Religions the Monopoly on Religion" *Journal of Ecumenical Studies* 11 (1974): 15-21.

________. "Hindu Ecclesial Consciousness- Some Ecclesiological Reflection" *Jeevadhara* 21 (May-June: 1974): 199-206.

________. "Samdhya the Vedic Prayer" *Indian Theological Studies* XIV/ 1 (March-1977): 22-38.

________. "Rtatattva: A Preface to a Hindu Christian Theology" *Jeevadhara* IX/ 49 (January-February: 1979): 6-63.

________. "Hermeneutics of Comparative Religion" *Journal of Dharma* 5/ 1 (January-March: 1980): 38-51.

________. "Man and Religion: A Dialogue with Panikkar" *Jeevadhara* 11/ 61 (January-February: 1981): 5-32.

________. "Towards an Ecumenical Ecumenism (Editorial)" *Journal of Ecumenical Studies* 19 (1982): 782-784.

________. "Cosmotheandric Intuition" *Jeevadhara* 14/ 79 (January-1984): 27-35.

________. "Towards an Ecumenical Theandric Spirituality" *Journal of Ecumenical Studies* 5/ 2 (Summer-1986): 501-513.

________. "Indic Theological Series" *Jeevadhara* XVII/ 101 (September-1987): 416-422.

________. "Christendom, Christianity, Christianness" Jeevadhara 21/ 124 (July-1991): 324-330.

________. "Neither Christo-monism nor Christo-dualism" *Jeevadhara* 14/142 (July-1994): 336-338.

________. "Indian Christian Theology" *Jeevadhara* XXVII/ 161 (September-1997): 319-321.

________. "Christology and Christophany" *Third Millennium* II (October-December: 1999): 10-22.

________. "Nine Sutra on the Asian Christ" *Jeevadhara* XXX/ 177 (May-2000): 330-334.

________. "The Encounter of Religions: The Unavoidable Dialogue" *Jnanadeepa* 3/2 (July-2000): 151-176.

________. "A Religious Meditation on Ayodhya" *Journal of Dharma* 25/ 1 (March-2000): 18-21.

________. "A New Society for a New Millennium" *Journal of Dharma* XXVII/1 (March-2002): 4-10.

II. Secondary Sources (Works on Panikkar)

Books

Joseph, Prabhu. (ed.), *The Intercultural Challenge of Raimon Panikkar* New York: Orbis Books, 1996.

Veliath, Dominic. *Theological Approach and Understanding of Religions- Jean Danielou and Raimundo Panikkar: A Study in Contrast* Bangalore: Kristu Jyoti College, 1988.

Articles

Gobb, John B. "Mystical Pluralism" in Joseph Prabhu (ed.), *The Inter-cultural Challenge of Raimon Panikkar* New York: Orbis Books, 1996.

D'Sa, Francis X. "The Notion of God" in Joseph Prabhu (ed.), *The Intercultural Challenge of Raimon Panikkar*, 1996.

________. "The Advaitic Principle of Raimon Panikkar and Trinity" in Patrick Gnanaprakasam and Elizabeth S. Fiorenza (eds.), *Negotiating Borders: Theological Explorations in the Global Era* Delhi: ISPCK, 2008.

Journals

Banon, Brad. "The Eco-Pneumatology of Raimon Panikkar" *Journal of Dharma* 31/ 4 (October-December: 2006): 457-472.

Cousins, E. H. "Trinity and the World Religions" *Journal of Ecumenical Studies* 7 (1970): 475-483.

D'Sa, Francis X. "The Interreligious Dialogue of the Future: Exploration into the Cosmotheandric Nature of Dialogue" *VJTR* 61/ 10 (October- 1997): 693-707.

Karokaran, Anto. "Raimond Panikkar's Theology of Religions: A Critique" *Indian Missiological Review* 12/2 (June-1996): 20-28.

________. "Raymond Panikkar's Theology of Religions: A Critique" *VJTR* LXIII/10 (October-1994): 663-672.

Nayak, Biren Kumar. "A Critical Study of Christology of Raimundo Panikkar in an Advaitic Frame Work" *Bangalore Theological Forum* 38/ 2 (December-2006): 196-212.

Parapally, Jacob. "Christophany: R Panikkar's Insight into Mystery of Christ" *Jeevadhara* 35/207 (May-2005): 253-264.

Reetz, Dankfreed. "R. Panikkar's Theology of Religions" *Religion and Society* XV/3 (September-1968): 32-54.

Savari Raj, Anthoni L. "The End of Reality: Raimon Panikkar's Cosmotheandric Vision and Its Implications." *JICPR* XXIV/ 1 (January-March: 2007): 132-139.

________. "The Diatopical Hermeneutics: R Panikkar's Response to the Scientific Study of Religions" *Journal of Dharma* 21/ 2 (April-June: 1996): 198-203.

Veliath, Dominic. "Christ and Religious Pluralism- Raimundo Panikkar" *Jeevadhara* 28/ 165 (May-1998): 207-220.

________. "From Ontonomy to Dialogical Dialogue: A Passacoglia" *VJTR* 5/ 1 (March-2002): 193-210.

________. "Raimundo Panikkar- A Pilgrimage to Contemporary Ecclesiological Consciousness" *Kristu Jyoti* 5/ 1 (March- 1989): 8-25.

________."The Trinity in Indian Theology" *Kristu Jyoti* 8/ 2 (June-1992): 1-24.

III. Other Sources

Dictionaries/Encyclopedias

Crooke, W. "Hinduism" in James Hastings (ed.), *Encyclopaedia of Religion and Ethics,* Vol. VI. Edinburgh: T&T Clark, 1974.

Fyffe, David. "Spirituality" in James Hastings (ed.), *Encyclopaedia of Religion and Ethics,* Vol. 11. Edinburgh: T&T Clark, 1974.

Larkin, E. E. "Christian Spirituality" in William J. McDonald (ed.), *New Catholic Encyclopaedia* London/Sydney: Mc Grow Hill Book Co., 1967.

Mather George A. and Larry A. Nicholas, *Dictionary of Cults, Sects, Religions and the Occults* Edinburgh: T&T Clark, 1993.

Wakefield, Gordon S. "Spirituality" in G. S. Wakefield (ed.), The Dictionary of Christian Spirituality London: SCM Press, 1983.

Books

Abraham, K. C. (ed.), *Third World Theologies: Commonalities and Divergences* Bangalore: EATWOT, 1995.

Aleaz, K. P. *Christian Thought through Advaita Vedanta* Delhi: ISPCK, 1996.

________. *Dimension of Indian Religion: Study, Experience and Interaction* Calcutta: Punti Pustak, 1995.

Balasundaram, F. J. *EATWOT in Asia* Bangalore: ATC, 1993.

Boyd, Robin. *An Introduction to Indian Christian Theology* Revised Edition. New Delhi: ISPCK, 2004.

________. *Khrist Advaita: A Theology for India* Madras: CLS, 1977.

Chatterjee, Margaret. *The Concept of Spirituality* New Delhi: Allied Publisher, 1989.

Deshpande, V. W. *The Impact of Ancient Indian Thought on Christianity* Delhi: A. P. H. Publishing Corp., 1996.

Ferm, William Deane. *Third World Liberation Theologies: An Introductory Survey* New York: Orbis Books, 1986.

Gamaliel, James Canjanam. *Dharma in the Hindu Scriptures and in the Bible* Delhi: ISPCK, 1997.

Guha, Ranajith and Gayatri, Chakravarthy (eds.). *Selected Subaltern Studies* New Delhi: Oxford University Press, 1988.

Hunt, Anne. *Trinity* New York: Orbis Books, 2005.

Illathuparampil, Mathew. (ed.), *The Contemporary Theologians: Context and Contributions* Bangalore: ATC, 2006.

Ivy. *Voices from Narmada: Doing Eco-feminist Theology* New Delhi: ISPCK, 2009.

Karokaran, Anto. *Evangelization and Diakonia: A Study in the Indian Perspective* Bangalore: Dharmaram Publication, 1978.

Knitter, Paul F. *No Other Name* Philippines: Claretian Publications, n.y.

Kyung, C. H. *Struggle to be the Sun Again: Introducing Asian Women's Theology* New York: Orbis Books, 1990.

Manimala, Varghese. *Towards Mutual Fecundation and Fulfilment* Delhi: Media House/ISPCK, 2009.

McGrath, Alister E. *Christian Theology: An Introduction* 2nd Edition. Oxford: Blackwell Publishers, 1997.

Mundadan, A. M. *Paths of Indian Theology* Bangalore: Dharmaram Publications, 1998.

Nalunakkal, George Mathew. *New Beings and New Communities: Theological Reflection in a Modern Context* Thiruvalla: KCC/ EDTP, 1998.

Narendranand, Swamy. *Hindu Spirituality* Sultanpur, UP: Jyoti Ashram, n.y.

Ogden, M. *Doing Theology Today* Pennsylvania: Trinity Press, 1996.

Pinto, Joseph P. *Introduction through Basic Communities: An Indian Perspective* Bangalore: ATC, 1985.

Radhakrishnan, S. *An Idealist View of Life* 2nd Edition London: Allen and Unwin, 1951.

Schwarz, Hans. *Theology in a Global Context* Michigan: Grand Rapids, 2005.

Sumithra, Sunand. *Christian Theologies from an Indian Perspective* Bangalore: TBT, 2002.

Tennet, Timothy C. *Building Christianity on Indian Foundations* Delhi: ISPCK, 2000.

Thumma, Anthoniraj. *Breaking Barriers: Liberation of Dialogue and Dialogue of Liberation* Delhi: ISPCK, 2000.

Wilfred, Felix. *Beyond Settled Foundations: The Journey of Indian Theology* Madras: University of Madras, 1993.

________. *From the Dusty Soil: Contextual Reinterpretation of Christianity* Madras: University of Madras, 1995.

________. *Margins: Site of Asian Theologies* Delhi: ISPCK, 2008.

________. *Sun Set in the East-Asian Challenges and Christian Involvement* Madras: University of Madras, 1991.

Williams, Rowan. *On Christian Theology: Christian Theology: Challenges in Contemporary Theology* Malden: Blackwell, 2000.

Young, Amos. *Hospitality and the Other: Pentecost, Christian Practices and the Neighbour* New York: Orbis Books, 2008.

Articles

Anand, S. "Mahisa-Mardana: A Myth of Holistic Liberation Theology" in Paul Puthanangady (ed.), *Towards Indian Theology of Liberation* Bangalore: Indian Theological Association, 1986.

Anand, Subash. "The Liberative Potential of Popular Religious Traditions" in David C. Scott and Israel Selvanayagam (eds.), *Re-visioning India's Religious Traditions* Delhi: ISPCK, 1996.

Ayrookuzhiel, A. M. A. "Dalit Theology: A Movement of Counter Culture" in James Massey (ed.), *Indigenous People: Dalits* Delhi: ISPCK, 1994.

Boyd, R. "Beyond Captivity" in Israel Selvanayagam (ed.), *Moving Forms of Theology: Faith Talk's Changing Contexts* Delhi: ISPCK, 2002.

Carr, Dayanchand. "A Biblical Basis for Dalit Theology" in James Massey (ed.), *Indigenous People: Dalit* Delhi: ISPCK, 1994.

Chatterjee, Salish C. "Hindu Religious Thought" in Kenneth Morgan (ed.), *The Religion of Hindus* Delhi: Motilal Banarsidass, 1986.

Chethimattam, John B. "Problem of an Indian Theology: A Critique of Indian Theologizing" in M. Amaladoss, T. K. John and G. Gilpert Sauch (eds.), *Theologizing in India* Bangalore: TPI, 1981.

Clarke, S. "Subalterns, Identity Politics and Christian Theology in India" in Sebastian C. H. Kim (ed.), *Christian Theology in Asia* New York: Cambridge University Press, 2008.

Devasia, M. A. "Sbalternity and Hermeneutic of Religious Language" in George Thadathil (ed.), *Subaltern Perspectives: Philosophizing in Context* Bangalore: ATC, 2005.

Gispert, Sauch G. "Karma." in G. Gispert Sauch (ed.), *Gems from India* Delhi: ISPCK, 2006.

Karotenprel, Sebastian. "Inter-Religious Dialogue" in Roger E. Hedlund and Paul Joshua Bhakiaraj *Missiology for the 21st Century* Delhi: ISPCK, 2004.

Lott, Eric J. "Hindu Theology's Forgotten Struggles" in Israel Selvanayagam (ed.), *Moving Forms of Theology: Faith Talk's Changing Contexts* Delhi: ISPCK, 2002.

Louis, Prakash. "The Meaning of Subaltern: A Socio-Philosophical Discourse" in George Thadathil (ed.), *Subaltern Perspectives: Philosophizing in Context* Bangalore: ATC, 2005.

__________. *Religious Faith, Human Identity: Dangerous Dynamics in Global and Indian Life* Bangalore: ATC/UTC, 2005.

Maher, J. Michael. "Agents of Dharma in a Worth Indian Village" in J. M. Maher (ed.), *The Untouchables in Contemporary India* New Delhi: Rawat Publications, 1998.

Marshall, Bruce D. "Trinity." in Gareth Jones (ed.), *The Blackwell Companion to Modern Theology* UK: Blackwell Publishing, 2007.

Minz, Nirmal. "Dalit-Tribal: A Search for Common Ideology" in A. P. Nirmal (ed.), *Towards Common Dalit Theology* Madras: Gurukul Publications, 1992.

Nehring, Andreas. "The Prodigal Son's Religious Grounding: Questioning Pluralistic Theologies" in David. C. Scott and Israel Selvanayagam (eds.), *Re-visioning India's Religious Traditions* Delhi: ISPCK, 1996.

Nirmal, A. P. "Doing Theology from a Dalit Perspective" in A. P. Nirmal (ed.), *A Reader in Dalit Theology* Madras: Gurukul Publications, 1989.

________. "Towards a Christian Theology" in James Massey (ed.), *Indigenous People: Dalits* Delhi: ISPCK, 1994.

Oddie, G. A. "The Dynamics of Popular Religion within Hinduism-The Case of Hook- Swinging Rituals" in David. C. Scott and Israel Selvanayagam (eds.), *Re-visioning India's Religious Traditions* Delhi: ISPCK, 1996.

Patrick, Gnana. "Subaltern Religions and Spirituality" in George Thadathil (ed.), *Subaltern Perspectives: Philosophizing in Context* Bangalore: ATC Publications, 2005.

Puthenpurackal, Johnson. "Philosophizing from the Dalit Perspective" in George Thadathil (ed.), *Subaltern Perspectives: Philosophizing in Context* Bangalore: ATC Publications, 2005.

Rao, C. H. Srinivasa. "The Three Margas of Salvation in Indian Christian Theology" in Anand Amaladoss (ed.), *Christian Contribution to Indian Philosophy* Madras: CLS, 1995.

Said, Edward W. "Forward" in Ranajit Guha and Gayatri Chakravarthy (eds.), *Selected Subaltern Studies* New Delhi: Oxford University, 1988.

Selvanayagam, Israel. "Water of Life and Indian Cups: Protestant Attempts at Theologizing in India" in Sebastian C. H. Kim (ed.), *Christian Theology in Asia* New York: Cambridge University Press, 2008.

Valiaveettil, Chacko. "The Influence of Advaitic Hinduism on Christianity" in Gnana Robinson (ed.), *Influence in Hinduism on Christianity* Madras: TTS Publications, 1980.

Wilfred, Felix. "The Problem of a Valid Starting Point for Theologizing in India" in M. A. Amaladoss, T. K. John and G. Gipert Sauch (eds.), *Theologizing in India* Bangalore: TPI, 1981.

Journals

Abraham, K. C. "Re-Interpretation of Christian Tradition in Contemporary India" *AJT* 9/ 2 (October-1995): 263-274.

Aleaz, K. P. "The Contributions of Advaita Vedanta to Indian Christian Theology in the Second Millennium" *Jeevadhara* XXIX/ 173 (September-1999): 355-369.

________. "Some Features of a Dalit Theology" *AJT* 18/ 1 (April-2004): 146-167.

________. "The Convergence of Dalit-Advaitic Theologies: An Exploration" *Indian Journal of Theology* 36/ 1 (1994): 97-108.

Alfara, Juan. "God Protects and Liberates the Poor- OT" *Concilium* (October-1986): 28-33.

Amaladoss, M. "Double Religious Belonging and Liminality" *VJTR* 66/ 1 (January-2002): 21-34.

________. "Proclaiming the Gospel" *VJTR* 57/ 1 (January-1993): 26-32.

Amalraj, Ashwanth. "The Cosmotheandric Vision of Ecology: A Philosophical Enterprise" *Jnanodaya* 16 (June-2009): 119-136.

Arapura, John G. "Re-Thinking Christianity in India: An Assessment of Indian Attempts" *Jeevadhara* XXIII/ 136 (July-1993): 284-290.

Ariarajah, Wesley. "Asian Christian Theological Task in the Midst of Other Religious Traditions" *CTC Bulletin* XVIII/ 1 (April-2002): 14-30.

Arulsamy, S. "Liberation Theology in India" *Indian Theological Studies* 22/ 3 (September-1985): 266-288.

Balasundaram, F. J. "Dalit Struggle and Its Implications for Theological Education" *Bangalore Theological Forum* XXIX/ 3, 4 (September-December: 1997): 71-79.

Callewaert, W. M. "God in Early Hindu Bhakti: Male and Female" *Journal of Dharma* 5/ 2 (April-June: 1980): 190-198.

Chatterjee, Saral K. "Indigenous Christianity and Counter Culture" *Religion and Society* XXXVI/ 4 (December-1989): 3-17.

Chethimattam, John B. "Religious Monograms and Mantras" *Journal of Dharma* IX/ 2 (April-June: 1984): 142-149.

Chung, Paul. "Trinity and Asian Theology of Divine Dukkar" *AJT* 16/ 1 (April-2002): 131-147.

Clarke, S. "Constructive Christian Theology: A Contextual Indian Proposal" *Bangalore Theological Forum* XXIV/ 1, 2 (March-June: 1997): 94-111.

________. "Dalit Christian Worship: A Theological Reflection" *Masihi Sevak* XXII/ 4 (December-1997): 14-23.

________. "Dalit Religion as a Resourceful Symbolic Domain: A Critical Review of Theories of Religion and a Constructive Proposition to Glean the Riches of Dalit Subjectivity" *Religion and Society* 49/ 2, 3 (June-September: 2004): 30-48.

DeSmet, R.V. "Categories of Indian Philosophy and Communication of the Gospel" *Religion and Society* 10/ 3 (September-1963): 20-26.

________. "Towards a Real Life-Indian Theology- The Advaita of Christianity" *VJTR* LIX/ 6 (June-1995): 405-409.

Dockhorn, K. "Christ in Hinduism as Seen in Recent Indian Theology" *Religion and Society* XXI/ 4 (December-1974): 39-47.

Dubey, S. P. "The Indian View of Life" *NCCR* CIII/ 9 (September-1983): 425-435.

Edanad, Antony. "Interiorized Word and Transforming Spirit: Johannine Model of Spirituality" *Journal of Dharma* XIII/ 3 (July-September: 1998): 238-247.

Elizabeth. "Liberative Spirituality and Feminist Models of Ecclesia as Resource for a Dalit Model of the Church" *NCCR* CXVIII/ 6 (June-July: 1998): 401-412.

Fernandes, Lionel. "Changing Perceptions of Indian Christians" *JPRS* 2/ 2 (July-1999): 149-163.

Fernandes, Walter. "Inter Religious Dialogue from the Perspective of Poor" *VJTR* 59/ 2 (February-1995): 91-105.

Hedlund, Roger E. "Subaltern Movements and Indian Churches of Indigenous Origins" *Journal of Dharma* XXIII/ 1 (January-March: 1998): 8-38.

Heredia, Rudolf E. "Subaltern Interrogations of Hindu Nationalism I" *VJTR* 66/ 10 (October-2002): 822-835.

________. "Subaltern Interrogations of Hindu Nationalism II" *VJTR* 66/ 11 (November-2002): 914-922.

Hoefer, Herbert. "Jesus My Master: Jesu Bhakta Hindu Christian Theology" *Dharma Deepika* 8/1 (January-June: 2004): 5-10.

Jathna, O.V. "Religious Pluralism- A Theological Critique" *Bangalore Theological Forum* 31/ 2 (December-1999): 1-19.

Jeremiah, Anderson. "Inculturation: A Subaltern Critique of K. P. Aleaz' Indian Christian Vedanta" *AJT* 21/ 2 (October-2007): 398-411.

Klostermaier, Klaus. "Sadhana- Sketch of Indian Spirituality" *Religion and Society* XVI/ 2 (June-1969): 36-50.

Knitter, Paul. "Cosmic Confidence or Preferential Option" *Bangalore Theological Forum* XXIII/ 4 (December-1991): 20-27.

Kolencherry, Antony. "South Indian Contribution to Sub-alternative Theologies" *Indian Theological Studies* XL/ 2 (June-2003): 125-141.

________. "Nishkama Karma- An Indian Paradigm for New Social order" *Indian Theological Studies* XXXVI/ 1 (March-1999): 5-20.

Lobo, Lancy. "Caste Dynamics" *Jeevadhara* XI/ 63 (May-June: 1981): 183-202.

________. "Towards an Inculturation in the Non- Sanskrit Tradition" *VJTR* 49/ 1 (January-1985): 16-28.

Madha, William. "Sakti: The Feminine Aspect of God in Indian Tradition" *Journal of Dharma* V/ 2 (April-June: 1980): 175-189.

Massey, James. "Need of a Dalit Theology" *CTC Bulletin* XVII/ 2 (April- 2001): 70-75.

Mattam, Joseph. "Witnessing to Christ through a Relevant Theological Language: An Indian Approach to a New Language in Theology" *Jeevadhara* XXXV/ 207 (May-2005): 181-199.

Mookenthottam, Antony. "Ground Work for an Indian Christian Theology" *Journal of Dharma* XIV/ 4 (October-December: 1989): 343-352.

Moses, Brindavan C. "Brahmanism: A Hindrance to the Emergence of a Vibrant Civil Society and the Establishment of Human Rights and Dignity for Dalits, Tribals and Women in India" *Religion and Society* 47/ 3 (September-2000): 41-51.

Mundadan, A. M. "Hindu Christian Dialogue" *Jeevadhara* 5/ 2 (September-October: 1981): 375-394.

Nagaraja, Rao P. "A Contemporary Hindu Understanding of Salvation" *Bangalore Theological Forum* 5/ 2 (July-December: 1973): 31-38.

Niles, Damayanthi. "The Study of Popular Religions and Our Theological Task" *AJT* 18/ 1 (April- 2004): 212-219.

Pandikattu, Kuruvilla. "Advaitic Model of Pluralism for India: An Indian Christian Contribution" *JPRS* 1/ 1 (January-1998): 127-149.

Rayan, Samuel. "Outside the Gate, Sharing the Insult" J*eevadhara* XI/ 63 (May-June: 1981): 203-231.

Robertson, S. "Hindu Spirituality" *Religion and Society* 50/ 2 (June-2005): 1-23.

________. "Periyar E.V. Ramaswamy's Critique of Priestly Hinduism and Its Implications for Social Reforms" *Religion and Society* 49/ 2 (June-September: 2004): 10-29.

Sahayadhas, R. "Perspective in Christological Reconstructions: An Exploration of the Writings of Select Theologians" *Bangalore Theological Forum* XXXVIII/ 2 (December-2006): 103-153.

________. "Christian Theological Hermeneutics in Asia: Prospects and Problems in Constructing Contextual Theologies" *Bangalore Theological Forum* XXXV/ 1 (June-2003): 151-176.

Sauch, G. Gispert. "Review of Christ the Mystery in History: A Critical Study of the Christology of Panikkar, by Cherian Menacherry " *VJTR* 60/ 2 (December-1996): 899-900.

Sharma, A. "Can Christian Theology be Astika?" *Indian Journal of Theology* 37/ 2 (1994): 10-13.

Stephen, M. "A Dalit Christology" *Faith Theological Review* VI/ 2 (September-2003): 23-33.

Thomas, T. K. "Gospel, and Indian Intellectuals Today" *Religion and Society* XIV/ 4 (September-1967): 31-49.

Timm, Jeffry R. "Vallabha, Vaishnavism and the Western Hegemony of Indian Thought" *Journal of Dharma* XIV/ 1 (January-March: 1989): 6-36.

Vanlalauva, H. "God in the Contemporary Christian Thought" *Mizoram Theological Journal* 2/ 2 (July-December: 2000): 2-21.

Vekathanam, Mathew. "Mystery, Myth and History: Dimensions of Spirituality in the Context of Advaita" *Journal of Dharma* XIII/ 3 (July-September: 1998): 201-211.

Veliath, Dominic. "God and Religions- Indian Approaches" *Kristu Jyoti* 15/ 1 (March-1999): 38-71.

Von, Bruck M. "Advaita and Trinity" *Indian Theological Studies* XX/ 1 (March-1983): 37-60.

Werner, Joachim. "Karma Marga in the Ramayana" *Gurukul Journal of Theological Studies* 7/ 1, 2 (1996-97): 95-103.

Wilfred, Felix. "Subaltern Religious Experience" *Journal of Dharma* XXIII/ 1 (January-March: 1998): 57-75.

________. The Challenge of Folklore to Indian Theologizing" *Jeevadhara* XXIV/ 139 (January-1994): 60-80.

Document

Indian Theological Association, "Towards an Indian Christian Spirituality in a Pluralistic Context" in *VJTR,* 55/3 (March-1991): 162-170.

Webliography

http://en.wikipedia.orgwiki/Raimon_Panikkar. 01 20, 2010.